Better Homes and Gardens®

CHRISTMAS COOKING
FROM THE HEART™

Taste the Season

Meredith® Consumer Marketing
Des Moines, Iowa

CHRISTMAS COOKING
FROM THE HEART™

MEREDITH CORPORATION CONSUMER MARKETING
Consumer Marketing Product Director: Heather Sorensen
Consumer Marketing Product Manager: Janece Schwartzkopf
Consumer Marketing Billing/Renewal Manager: Tami Beachem
Business Director: Ron Clingman
Senior Production Manager: Al Rodruck
Photographers: Jacob Fox, Jason Donnelly

WATERBURY PUBLICATIONS, INC.
Editorial Director: Lisa Kingsley
Creative Director: Ken Carlson
Associate Editors: Tricia Bergman, Annie Peterson
Associate Design Director: Doug Samuelson
Graphic Designer: Mindy Samuelson
Contributing Copy Editor: Peg Smith
Contributing Proofreader: Terri Fredrickson
Contributing Indexer: Mary Williams
Contributing Food Stylists: Jennifer Peterson, Charlie Worthington
Contributing Prop Stylist: Sue Mitchell

BETTER HOMES AND GARDENS® MAGAZINE
Editor in Chief: Gayle Goodson Butler
Art Director: Michael D. Belknap
Senior Deputy Editor: Nancy Wall Hopkins
Editorial Assistant: Renee Irey

MEREDITH PUBLISHING GROUP
President: Tom Harty

MEREDITH CORPORATION
Chairman and Chief Executive Officer: Stephen M. Lacy

In Memoriam: E.T. Meredith III (1933–2003)

Better Homes and Gardens®
Test Kitchen

Our seal assures you that every recipe in *Christmas Cooking from the Heart*™ has been tested in the Better Homes and Gardens® Test Kitchen. This means that each recipe is practical and reliable and it meets our high standards of taste appeal. We guarantee your satisfaction with this book for as long as you own it.

All of us at Meredith® Consumer Marketing are dedicated to providing you with information and ideas to enhance your home. We welcome your comments and suggestions. Write to us at: Meredith Consumer Marketing, 1716 Locust St., Des Moines, IA 50309-3023. *Christmas Cooking from the Heart*™ is available by mail. To order editions from past years, call 800/627-5490.

Cover Photography: Jason Donnelly
Front cover: Vanilla Holiday Cookies (page 103)

PEAR DUMPLINGS
WITH MAPLE-
ORANGE SAUCE,
PAGE 85

GARLIC
ROSEMARY
DRESSING,
PAGE 145

Table of Contents

Taste the Season

CERTAIN FLAVORS AND SCENTS are associated with this very special time of year—the aromatic spice of nutmeg-topped eggnog, the lip-tingling taste of peppermint, savory sage-infused stuffing. Some of the best holiday memories are made at the table or in the kitchen, surrounded by family and friends. Tried-and-true favorites are a familiar comfort, while wonderful new recipes add excitement to the season. Good food draws people together and spreads joy. That's what *Better Homes and Gardens® Christmas Cooking from the Heart™* is all about—providing recipes and ideas that will help you create wonderful experiences this Christmas and memories for holidays to come. For a big family feast, try Maple-Sage Turkey (page 10) or Cajun-Spiced Ham (page 12). For a celebratory holiday brunch, try Smoked Salmon Eggs Benedict (page 46) or Amaretto Brioche Bake (page 53). And, of course, Christmas would not be complete without cookies—from Chocolate-Cherry Thumbprints (page 104) to Danish Pastry Apple Bars (page 110).

Happy Cooking—and Happy Holidays!

Around the Table

WITH ALL OF THE wonderful food enjoyed during the holiday season, the Christmas feast is the highlight. Create a memory-making meal for family and friends from these recipes for main dishes, salads, soups, sides, and breads.

CAJUN-SPICED HAM,
PAGE 12

Maple Sage Turkey

THAW 4 days PREP 30 minutes
ROAST 2 hours 40 minutes at
450°F/350°F STAND 15 minutes
MAKES 18 servings

- 1 14-pound frozen turkey
- 3 tablespoons coarse kosher salt
- 3 tablespoons maple sugar or packed brown sugar
- 1 teaspoon dried sage, crushed
- ½ teaspoon freshly ground black pepper
- 2 cups hot water
- ½ cup maple syrup
- ¼ cup unsalted butter
- 4 teaspoons finely shredded orange peel
- 1 teaspoon ground chipotle chile pepper
- 1 teaspoon whole black peppercorns

1. Partially thaw turkey in the refrigerator for 1 to 2 days or until breast meat gives when pressed (turkey will be somewhat frozen). Remove turkey from packaging; pat dry.
2. For rub, in a small bowl mix salt, sugar, dried sage, and black pepper; rub over turkey. Place turkey, breast side up, on a rack in a large roasting pan. Cover loosely with plastic wrap. Refrigerate for 3 days or until fully thawed. Remove plastic wrap.
3. Preheat oven to 450°F. Remove neck and giblets from turkey cavity. Loop kitchen string around drumsticks; tie securely to tail. Pour the hot water into roasting pan with turkey. Reduce heat to 350°F. Roast turkey, uncovered, for 2 hours. (If breast browns too quickly, cover loosely with foil.)

4. For glaze, in a small saucepan heat maple syrup, butter, orange peel, chipotle, and peppercorns until warm. After 2 hours of roasting, generously brush turkey with glaze every 20 minutes for 40 to 60 minutes or until meat thermometer inserted in the thigh (not touching bone) registers at least 175°F. Remove turkey from oven. Tent loosely with foil; let stand 15 minutes. Reserve drippings for gravy.
PER SERVING 407 cal., 16 g fat (5 g sat. fat), 186 mg chol., 1,197 mg sodium, 10 g carb., 1 g fiber, 55 g pro.

Turkey Gravy

PREP 30 minutes
ROAST 1 hour at 400°F
COOK 1 hour MAKES 24 servings

- 6 stalks celery, cut up
- 4 carrots, unpeeled and cut up
- 2 onions, unpeeled and quartered
- 2 tablespoons unsalted butter, melted
- 5 pounds bone-in, skin-on turkey thighs or drumsticks
- ½ cup dry white wine
- 8 cups water
- 1 tablespoon whole black peppercorns
- 2 bay leaves
- ½ cup unsalted butter
- ½ cup all-purpose flour
- ¼ cup cornstarch
- ¼ cup cold water
- 1 cup reserved Maple Sage Turkey drippings
   Salt and pepper
   Marjoram leaves (optional)

1. For turkey broth, preheat oven to 400°F. Place celery, carrots, and onions in a roasting pan; add 2 tablespoons melted butter and toss to coat. Top vegetables with turkey. Roast turkey pieces and vegetables uncovered, for 1 hour.

2. Remove turkey and vegetables to an 8-quart stockpot. Stir the wine into hot roasting pan; scrape up browned bits. Add to stockpot with vegetable and turkey. Add the 8 cups water to the stockpot; add peppercorns and bay leaves. Bring water to boiling; reduce heat and simmer, covered, for 1 hour.
3. Use a slotted spoon to remove turkey and vegetables from broth. Strain broth through a fine-mesh sieve; discard solids. Measure 6 cups broth. Cover and chill or freeze remaining broth for another use.
4. In a 4-quart stockpot melt ½ cup butter over medium heat. When it foams add the flour and whisk until smooth. Reduce heat to medium-low; cook for 10 minutes, stirring frequently, until flour darkens to a deep caramel color. Remove from heat. Carefully stir in broth.
5. In a small bowl stir together the cornstarch and the cold water. Add to stockpot; cook and stir until thickened and bubbly. Cook and stir 2 minutes more. Add the drippings from Maple Sage Turkey, then season to taste with salt and pepper. If desired, stir in marjoram leaves before serving.
PER ¼ CUP 67 cal., 5 g fat (3 g sat. fat), 16 mg chol., 53 mg sodium, 4 g carb., 0 g fiber, 1 g pro.

MAPLE SAGE
TURKEY AND
TURKEY GRAVY

Cajun-Spiced Ham

PREP 15 minutes
ROAST 1½ hours at 325°F
MAKES 20 servings

- 1 tablespoon packed brown sugar
- 1 tablespoon garlic powder
- 1 tablespoon onion powder
- 1 tablespoon dried oregano, crushed
- 1 tablespoon dried thyme, crushed
- 1 tablespoon paprika
- 1 to 2 teaspoons cayenne pepper
- 1 teaspoon salt
- 1 teaspoon dried lemon peel
- 1 teaspoon black pepper
- 1 6- to 8-pound cooked ham, rump half
  Pure maple syrup (optional)
- 1 orange, halved and seared (optional)

1. Preheat oven to 325°F. For rub, in a small bowl combine brown sugar, garlic powder, onion powder, oregano, thyme, paprika, cayenne pepper, salt, lemon peel, and black pepper. Sprinkle over ham; rub in with your fingers.
2. Place ham on a rack in a shallow roasting pan. Insert an oven-going thermometer into center of ham; thermometer should not touch bone.
3. Place roasting pan on oven rack. Pour enough water into the roasting pan to reach ½ inch up sides of pan. Cover with foil; roast for 1 hour. Remove foil. Roast for 30 minutes to 1¼ hours more or until thermometer registers 140°F. If desired, serve ham with maple syrup and seared orange halves.

PER SERVING *248 cal., 13 g fat (4 g sat. fat), 84 mg chol., 1,100 mg sodium, 3 g carb., 0 g fiber, 31 g pro.*

Herbed Tri-Tip Roast with Demi-Glace

PREP 40 minutes
ROAST 30 minutes at 425°F
COOK 40 minutes   STAND 15 minutes
MAKES 8 servings

- 1 teaspoon dried thyme, crushed
- ½ teaspoon salt
- ½ teaspoon coarsely ground black pepper
- 1 2-pound boneless beef tri-tip roast
- 1 tablespoon olive oil
- ½ cup chopped onion
- ½ cup sliced carrot
- 1 teaspoon sugar
- ¼ cup butter
- 4 teaspoons all-purpose flour
- 1 14.5-ounce can beef broth
- 2 tablespoons tomato paste
- ½ teaspoon dried thyme, crushed
- 1 bay leaf
- ⅛ teaspoon black pepper

1. Preheat oven to 425°F. In a small bowl combine the thyme, salt, and pepper. Rub all over meat. Place meat on a rack in a shallow roasting

CAJUN-SPICED
HAM

pan. Drizzle with olive oil. Roast, uncovered, for 30 to 35 minutes or until an instant-read thermometer registers 135°F for medium rare or 150°F for medium.

2. Meanwhile, prepare Demi-Glace. In a medium saucepan cook onion, carrot, and sugar in butter over medium-low heat for 15 minutes or until tender and starting to brown, stirring occasionally. Stir in the flour. Cook for 5 minutes more or until flour is brown. Add broth, tomato paste, thyme, bay leaf, and pepper. Bring to boiling; reduce heat and simmer, uncovered, for 20 to 25 minutes or until reduced to about 1½ cups, stirring occasionally. Strain through a fine-mesh sieve; discard vegetables and bay leaf.

3. Remove roast from oven. Cover with foil; let stand 15 minutes. (Meat temperature will rise 10°F during standing time). Slice beef and serve with Demi-Glace.

PER SERVING *282 cal., 18 g fat (8 g sat. fat), 92 mg chol., 366 mg sodium, 5 g carb., 0 g fiber, 24 g pro.*

Black-Eyed Pea Relish

PREP **15 minutes** CHILL **1 hour**
MAKES **12 servings**

- ¼ cup diced red onion
- 1 yellow sweet pepper, seeded and diced
- ½ of a red sweet pepper, seeded and diced
- ½ of a green sweet pepper, seeded and diced
- 1 serrano chile pepper*, thinly sliced
- 1 clove garlic, minced
- 2 roma tomatoes, diced
- 1 11-ounce package steamed ready-to-eat black-eyed peas, rinsed and drained; or one 15-ounce can black-eyed peas, rinsed and drained
- ¼ cup seasoned rice vinegar
  Sea salt and freshly ground pepper
- 1 roma tomato, sliced (optional)

1. In a large bowl gently combine onion, sweet peppers, chile pepper, garlic, diced tomatoes, black-eyed peas, and vinegar. Season to taste

with salt and pepper. Top with tomato slices, if desired. Chill for 1 hour to blend and for chiles to pickle.

PER SERVING *50 cal., 0 g fat, 0 mg chol., 72 mg sodium, 9 g carb., 2 g fiber, 3 g pro.*

***Tip** Chile peppers contain oils that can irritate your skin and eyes. Wear plastic or rubber gloves when working with them.

Pear-Cranberry Relish

PREP **10 minutes** COOK **15 minutes**
MAKES **16 servings**

- 1 12-ounce bag fresh cranberries
- ⅓ cup chopped onion
- 1 cup packed brown sugar
- ½ cup water
- 3 tablespoons lemon juice
- 1 1-inch piece fresh ginger, peeled and grated
- ¼ teaspoon ground cinnamon
- ⅛ teaspoon ground cloves
  Dash cayenne pepper
- 3 Bosc pears, cored and chopped

1. In a medium saucepan combine cranberries, onion, brown sugar, the water, lemon juice, ginger, cinnamon, cloves, and cayenne pepper. Bring to boiling; reduce heat. Simmer, uncovered, about 10 minutes or until cranberries soften. Add pears; cook for 5 to 10 minutes more or until pears are soft yet keep their shape. Serve at room temperature or chilled.

PER SERVING *83 cal., 0 g fat, 0 mg chol., 5 mg sodium, 22 g carb., 2 g fiber, 0 g pro.*

PEAR-CRANBERRY RELISH

LEMON-ROSEMARY
POTATO ROLLS

Two-Cheese Garlic and Herb Biscuits

PREP 20 minutes
BAKE 10 minutes at 450°F
MAKES 9 servings

- 1 cup all-purpose flour
- ½ cup white whole wheat flour or whole wheat flour
- 1 tablespoon snipped fresh basil or 1 teaspoon dried basil, crushed
- 2 teaspoons baking powder
- 2 cloves garlic, minced
- ¼ teaspoon cream of tartar
- ⅛ teaspoon salt
- 2 ounces soft goat cheese (chèvre) or reduced-fat cream cheese (Neufchâtel)
- 2 tablespoons butter
- ¼ cup finely shredded Parmesan cheese (1 ounce)
- ½ cup fat-free milk
  Milk
  Butter (optional)

1. Preheat oven to 450°F. In a medium bowl stir together all-purpose flour, whole wheat flour, basil, baking powder, garlic, cream of tartar, and salt. Using a pastry blender, cut in goat cheese and butter until mixture resembles coarse crumbs. Stir in 3 tablespoons of the Parmesan cheese. Make a well in the center of the flour mixture. Add milk all at once; stir just until dough clings together.
2. Turn out dough on a lightly floured surface. Knead by folding and gently pressing dough for four to six strokes or until nearly smooth. Pat or lightly roll dough into an 8×6-inch rectangle.
3. Cut dough into nine rectangles. Brush tops with milk and sprinkle with the remaining Parmesan cheese. Place biscuits 1 inch apart on an ungreased baking sheet. Bake for 10 to 12 minutes or until golden brown. If desired, brush tops with butter. Serve warm.

PER SERVING *127 cal., 5 g fat (3 g sat. fat), 12 mg chol., 171 mg sodium, 17 g carb., 1 g fiber, 5 g pro.*

Lemon-Rosemary Potato Rolls

PREP 45 minutes
CHILL 2 hours RISE 1 hour
BAKE 20 minutes at 375°F
MAKES 48 servings

- 2 tablespoons instant mashed potato flakes
- 2 cups boiling water
- ¾ cup unsalted butter, cubed
- ⅓ cup sugar
- 2 tablespoons finely chopped fresh rosemary leaves
- 2 teaspoons salt
- 2 tablespoon lemon zest
- 2 packages active dry yeast (1½ tablespoons)
- 4 large eggs
- 8 cups all-purpose flour
- 1 tablespoon whipping cream, half-and-half, or light cream
- 1 stick butter
- 1 tablespoon snipped fresh rosemary

1. In a large mixing bowl combine potato flakes and the boiling water. Mix in butter, sugar, rosemary, salt, and 1 tablespoon of the lemon zest. Let stand 10 minutes.
2. In small bowl sprinkle yeast over ¼ cup *warm water* (105°F to 115°F); stir to dissolve yeast. Let stand for 5 minutes or until foamy.
3. Whisk eggs into butter mixture, then the yeast mixture. Stir in flour, 2 cups at a time, until a thick, sticky dough forms.
4. Lightly grease two 13×9-inch pans or disposable foil pans. Turn dough out onto a floured surface; quickly pat dough into a large rectangle, about 12×16 inches. Use a floured knife to cut dough into 48 pieces. With floured hands, pull pieces into balls. Arrange side-by-side in prepared pans. Cover with plastic wrap; refrigerate for 2 hours or up to 3 days. Or, cover with plastic wrap then foil; freeze up to 1 month.
5. To bake, let dough rise at room temperature for 1 hour (about 2 hours for frozen dough) or until doubled. Preheat oven to 375°F. Brush roll tops with cream. Bake for 20 to 25 minutes or until browned. Serve warm with herbed lemon butter, if desired.
6. For the herbed lemon butter, let butter stand at room temperature 10 minutes. In a shallow dish combine remaining lemon zest and rosemary. Gently roll butter in lemon-rosemary. Wrap in plastic wrap. Cover and chill up to 1 week.

PER SERVING *118 cal., 4 g fat (2 g sat. fat), 24 mg chol., 104 mg sodium, 18 g carb., 1 g fiber, 3 g pro.*

SQUASH, MUSHROOM, AND FARRO DRESSING

APRICOT-PECAN STUFFING

Squash, Mushroom, and Farro Dressing

PREP 40 minutes
ROAST 25 minutes at 425°F
COOK 35 minutes
BAKE 20 minutes at 350°F
MAKES 10 servings

½ of a medium butternut squash, peeled, seeded, and cut into ½-inch cubes (2¾ cups)
2 tablespoons olive oil
3 cups halved fresh cremini and/or button mushrooms leave (mushrooms whole, if small)
6 cups water
1½ cups pearled farro
4 ounces thick sliced pancetta, chopped
¾ cup coarsely chopped onion
½ cup thinly sliced celery
3 cloves garlic, minced
¾ cup dry white wine
½ cup half-and-half or light cream
1 tablespoon snipped fresh thyme or 1 teaspoon dried thyme, crushed
2 teaspoons snipped fresh rosemary or ½ teaspoon dried rosemary, crushed
¾ teaspoon salt
¼ teaspoon freshly ground black pepper
½ cup finely shredded Asiago cheese (2 ounces)

1. Preheat oven to 425°F. Line a shallow baking pan with foil. In a large bowl toss together squash and 1 tablespoon of the oil. Transfer squash to the foil-lined baking pan. Roast for 10 minutes. Stir squash and push to one side of the pan. Toss mushrooms in remaining 1 tablespoon olive oil. Place mushrooms on opposite side of pan. Roast about 15 minutes or just until squash is tender and mushrooms are roasted. Reduce oven temperature to 350°F.
2. Meanwhile, in a large saucepan bring the water to boiling; add farro. Return to boiling; reduce heat. Simmer, covered, for 25 to 30 minutes or just until tender; drain.
3. In a very large skillet cook pancetta over medium-high heat until crisp. Drain pancetta on paper towels.

Add the onion, celery, and garlic to drippings in skillet. Cook over medium heat about 3 minutes or until vegetables are tender, stirring occasionally. Add wine, half-and-half, thyme, rosemary, salt, and pepper to skillet. Bring to boiling. Add squash to skillet and mash slightly for sauce-like consistency. Stir in cheese until melted. Stir in drained farro, mushrooms, and pancetta; toss to combine. Transfer dressing to a buttered 2-quart casserole or baking dish. Cover with foil.
4. Bake for 20 minutes or until heated through.

PER SERVING 251 cal., 10 g fat (4 g sat. fat), 14 mg chol., 334 mg sodium, 28 g carb., 3 g fiber, 10 g pro.

To Make Ahead: Prepare as directed, through Step 3. Refrigerate up to 24 hours. To bake, let stand at room temperature 30 minutes. Proceed with Step 4, baking about 30 minutes or until heated through.

Apricot-Pecan Stuffing

PREP 25 minutes
SLOW COOK 3½ hours (low)
MAKES 12 servings

Nonstick cooking spray
6 tablespoons butter
1 cup sliced leeks
1 cup chopped onion
2 cups peeled (if desired) and chopped apples, such as Braeburn, Jonathan, McIntosh, Rome Beauty, or Granny Smith
1 cup chopped pecans
¾ cup snipped dried apricots
1 teaspoon dried thyme, crushed
½ teaspoon salt
½ teaspoon ground nutmeg
⅛ teaspoon black pepper
12 cups dried 2-inch whole wheat or white bread cubes
1¾ to 2 cups chicken broth

1. Lightly coat a 5- to 6-quart slow cooker with cooking spray; set aside. In a large skillet melt butter over medium heat. Add leeks and onion; cook about 5 minutes or until tender, stirring occasionally. Stir in apples, pecans, dried apricots, thyme, salt, nutmeg, and pepper. Cook for 3 minutes, stirring occasionally.
2. In an extra-large bowl combine bread cubes and apple mixture. Drizzle with enough broth to moisten, toss lightly to combine. Transfer dressing to the slow cooker.
3. Cover and cook on low-heat setting for 3½ to 4 hours or until an instant-read thermometer inserted in center registers 165°F.

PER SERVING 254 cal., 14 g fat (5 g sat. fat), 16 mg chol., 450 mg sodium, 29 g carb., 5 g fiber, 7 g pro.

Herbed Wild Rice

PREP 25 minutes
SLOW COOK 6 hours (low) or
3 hours (high)
MAKES 12 servings

- 2 cups fresh white or brown button mushrooms, quartered
- 1 cup sliced carrots
- 1½ cups chopped onions
- 1 cup uncooked wild rice, rinsed and drained
- 1 cup uncooked brown rice
- 1 teaspoon dried basil, crushed
- ½ teaspoon dried thyme, crushed
- ½ teaspoon dried rosemary, crushed
- ¼ teaspoon black pepper
- 4 cloves garlic, minced
- 1 tablespoon butter or margarine
- 1 14.5-ounce can diced tomatoes, undrained
- 2 14-ounce cans vegetable or chicken broth
   Fresh snipped Italian parsley

1. In a 3½- or 4-quart slow cooker combine mushrooms, carrots, onions, wild rice, brown rice, basil, thyme, rosemary, pepper, garlic, and butter. Pour undrained tomatoes and broth over mixture in cooker.
2. Cover and cook on low-heat setting for 6 to 7 hours or on high-heat setting for 3 to 3½ hours. Stir before serving. Sprinkle with snipped parsley.
PER SERVING *141 cal., 2 g fat (1 g sat. fat), 3 mg chol., 345 mg sodium, 28 g carb., 3 g fiber, 4 g pro.*

Pumpkin Parmesan Risotto

PREP 20 minutes COOK 45 minutes
MAKES 4 servings

- 2 to 2½ cups water
- 1¾ cups chicken broth
- 3 tablespoons unsalted butter
- 1 cup finely chopped onion
- 1 clove garlic, minced
- 2 cups uncooked arborio rice
- 1 cup dry white wine
- 1½ tablespoons snipped fresh sage
- 1 cup Pumpkin Puree*
- ½ cup finely shredded Parmigiano-Reggiano cheese
   Shaved Parmigiano-Reggiano cheese (optional)
   Sage leaves (optional)

1. In a large saucepan bring the water and broth to boiling; reduce heat to maintain simmer.
2. In a heavy 4-quart saucepan melt butter over medium heat. Add onion and garlic; cook about 3 minutes or until tender, stirring occasionally. Add rice; cook and stir for 2 minutes. Add wine; cook and stir until liquid is absorbed. Stir in the snipped sage and about 1 cup simmering broth; stir until almost all of the liquid is absorbed. Continue cooking and adding broth, 1 cup at a time, stirring until almost all liquid is absorbed before adding more until rice is tender yet firm to the bite and risotto is creamy.
3. Stir Pumpkin Puree and the ½ cup cheese into risotto. Heat through about 1 minute. Serve in bowls. If desired, top with shaved cheese and sage leaves.
***Pumpkin Puree** Preheat oven to 375°F. Cut 2½ pounds pie pumpkins into 5×5-inch pieces. Remove and discard seeds and strings. Arrange pieces in a single layer, skin sides

HERBED
WILD RICE

up, in a foil-lined baking pan. Cover with foil. Bake about 1 hour or until tender. When cool enough to handle, scoop pulp from rind. Place pulp in food processor or blender. Cover and process or blend until smooth. Measure 1 cup puree for risotto. Transfer remaining puree to an airtight container. Refrigerate up to 3 days or freeze up to 6 months. Thaw frozen puree in the refrigerator.

PER SERVING *385 cal., 12 g fat (7 g sat. fat), 26 mg chol., 547 mg sodium, 61 g carb., 6 g fiber, 10 g pro.*

Orzo and Olive Salad with Spiced Citrus Vinaigrette

PREP 35 minutes CHILL 2 hours
MAKES 8 servings

- 1½ cups dried whole wheat or regular orzo pasta
- ½ cup orange juice
- ¼ cup snipped fresh mint
- ¼ cup lemon juice
- 2 tablespoons honey
- 1 tablespoon olive oil
- 1 teaspoon ground coriander
- 1 teaspoon grated fresh ginger
- ½ teaspoon salt
- ¼ teaspoon crushed red pepper
- ¼ teaspoon ground turmeric
- 2 cups lightly packed arugula
- 1 cup packaged julienned carrots
- ¾ cup thinly sliced green onions
- ½ cup pitted green olives, halved
- ½ cup golden raisins

1. In a large saucepan cook orzo according to package directions. Rinse with cold water to cool slightly; drain.
2. Meanwhile, in a large bowl whisk together orange juice, mint, lemon juice, honey, olive oil, coriander, ginger, salt, crushed red pepper, and turmeric. Add drained orzo, arugula, carrots, green onions, olives, and raisins. Stir until well combined. Cover and chill at least 2 hours or up to 24 hours.

PER SERVING *206 cal., 3 g fat (0 g sat. fat), 0 mg chol., 304 mg sodium, 40 g carb., 7 g fiber, 5 g pro.*

SHAVED FENNEL AND CELERY SALAD

Shaved Fennel and Celery Salad

START TO FINISH 20 minutes
MAKES 12 servings

- 6 tablespoons fresh lemon juice
- ⅓ cup extra virgin olive oil
- 2 tablespoons minced shallot
- ½ teaspoon sugar
- ½ teaspoon kosher salt
- ¼ teaspoon cracked black pepper
- 2 5-ounce packages torn mixed greens (about 9 cups)
- 5 stalks celery (including tops), thinly sliced (2½ cups)
- 2 medium fennel bulbs, trimmed, cored, and thinly sliced (2 cups)
- 4 ounces freshly shaved Parmesan cheese

1. In a small bowl whisk together lemon juice, olive oil, shallot, sugar, salt, and pepper; set aside.
2. In a very large bowl combine the greens, celery, fennel, and Parmesan cheese. Add dressing and toss gently to coat.

PER SERVING *108 cal., 9 g fat (2 g sat. fat), 7 mg chol., 271 mg sodium, 4 g carb., 1 g fiber, 4 g pro.*

CARAMELIZED VEGGIE
LENTIL SALAD

Caramelized Veggie Lentil Salad

PREP 40 minutes
ROAST 30 minutes at 425°F
CHILL 48 hours MAKES 21 servings

2½ pounds fennel bulbs, trimmed, cored, quartered, and thinly sliced (reserve fronds, if desired)
1 pound carrots, peeled and finely chopped
3 tablespoons unsalted butter, melted
   Salt and black pepper
2 cups dried French green lentils*
6 cloves garlic, minced
2 bay leaves
4 cups reduced-sodium chicken broth
½ teaspoon salt
½ cup extra virgin olive oil
3 tablespoons country Dijon mustard
1 tablespoon balsamic vinegar
1 tablespoon honey
2 cups loosely packed Italian parsley, finely chopped
⅓ cup finely chopped large shallots
¼ cup finely chopped large sage leaves

1. Preheat oven to 425°F. In a 15×10×1-inch baking pan toss fennel and carrots with melted butter; season generously with salt and pepper. Roast, uncovered, for 30 minutes or until tender and caramelized, stirring once or twice.
2. Meanwhile, wash and rinse the lentils. In a 4-quart saucepan combine lentils, garlic, bay leaves, and chicken broth; bring to boiling. Reduce heat and simmer, uncovered, for 20 to 25 minutes or until lentils are tender. Drain any remaining liquid from lentils. Remove and discard bay leaves. Stir in salt.
3. In a very large bowl whisk together the olive oil, mustard, balsamic vinegar, and honey. Stir in lentil mixture, parsley, shallots, and sage; stir in caramelized vegetables.
4. Serve immediately or cover and refrigerate up to 2 days. Serve cold or at room temperature. If desired, garnish with additional parsley and fennel fronds.
PER SERVING 165 cal., 7 g fat (2 g sat. fat), 4 mg chol., 316 mg sodium, 19 g carb., 8 g fiber, 7 g pro.
* Or substitute 6 cups packaged precooked lentils for the dry lentils and skip Step 2.

Citrus and Smoked Almond Salad

START TO FINISH 20 minutes
MAKES 16 servings

¼ cup fresh orange juice
3 tablespoons fresh lemon juice
¼ cup extra virgin olive oil
½ teaspoon kosher salt
¼ teaspoon cracked black pepper
2 5-ounce packages torn mixed greens
2 oranges, peeled, halved, and sliced (1 naval and 1 Cara Cara)
2 grapefruits, peeled and sectioned (1 cup)
¾ cup pomegranate seeds
¾ cup smoked almonds, coarsely chopped

1. For dressing, in a small bowl whisk together the orange juice, lemon juice, olive oil, salt, and pepper; set aside.
2. In a very large bowl combine the greens, oranges, grapefruits, pomegranate seeds, and almonds. Add dressing and gently toss.
PER SERVING 91 cal., 7 g fat (1 g sat. fat), 0 mg chol., 65 mg sodium, 7 g carb., 2 g fiber, 2 g pro.

CITRUS AND
SMOKED
ALMOND SALAD

Cheesy Mashed Potatoes with Gouda and Crispy Pancetta

START TO FINISH **40 minutes**
MAKES **8 servings**

1 pound red potatoes, cut into 1½-inch pieces
1 pound russet potatoes, peeled and cut into 1½-inch pieces
2 green onions
5 ounces pancetta, cut into ¼-inch cubes (about 1 cup)
¾ cup half-and-half, light cream, or whipping cream
2 cups finely shredded Gouda cheese (8 ounces)
Salt
Freshly ground black pepper

1. In a Dutch oven cook potatoes, covered, in enough lightly salted boiling water to cover for 20 to 25 minutes or until tender; drain. Return potatoes to Dutch oven.
2. Meanwhile, thinly slice green onions, separating the white portion from the green tops. Set green tops aside. In a medium skillet cook white portions of onions and the pancetta over medium-high heat about 8 minutes or until pancetta is crisp, stirring occasionally. Drain off fat.
3. Add half-and-half to cooked potatoes. Mash with a potato masher or mixer on low until nearly smooth. Stir in 1½ cups of the cheese and the pancetta mixture. Season to taste with salt and pepper.
4. Transfer mashed potatoes to a serving dish. Sprinkle with green onion tops and remaining ½ cup cheese.
PER SERVING *272 cal., 16 g fat (9 g sat. fat), 47 mg chol., 502 mg sodium, 21 g carb., 2 g fiber, 13 g pro.*
Make Ahead Prepare as directed through Step 3. Transfer mashed potatoes to a greased 2-quart baking dish. Cover and refrigerate up to 24 hours. Preheat oven to 350°F. Bake, covered with foil, for 40 to 45 minutes or until heated through.

Roasted Broccoli and Olives

PREP **15 minutes** STAND **5 minutes**
ROAST **20 minutes at 425°F**
MAKES **8 servings**

6 cloves garlic, peeled and gently crushed
1 teaspoon kosher salt, divided
¼ cup extra virgin olive oil, plus more for drizzling
2¼ to 2½ pounds broccoli, washed, drained, and patted dry
½ cup mixed unpitted olives
Flaked sea salt
½ of a lemon

1. Preheat oven to 425°F. Line a 15×10×1-inch baking pan with parchment paper; set aside. In a small bowl combine garlic and ½ teaspoon of the kosher salt. Using the back of a spoon, muddle garlic and salt until garlic begins to release its oil. Let stand for 5 to 10 minutes. Stir in oil.
2. Trim broccoli stems; cut stalks lengthwise into halves and/or quarters. Place in prepared baking pan. Pour over garlic oil and olives; toss well. Sprinkle with remaining kosher salt. Roast for 20 to 25 minutes, tossing occasionally, until tender-crisp. Transfer to a serving dish.
3. Squeeze lemon juice over broccoli, sprinkle with flaked sea salt, and drizzle with additional olive oil.
PER SERVING *134 cal., 10 g fat (1 g sat. fat), 0 mg chol., 427 mg sodium, 10 g carb., 4 g fiber, 4 g pro.*

CHEESY MASHED POTATOES WITH GOUDA AND CRISPY PANCETTA

Spice-and-Honey Roasted Carrots

PREP **20 minutes**
ROAST **25 minutes at 425°F**
MAKES **6 servings**

1½ pounds regular or tricolor carrots
  1 tablespoon olive oil
½ cup coarsely chopped hazelnuts (filberts)
  1 tablespoon coriander seeds
  1 tablespoon sesame seeds
1½ teaspoons cumin seeds
½ teaspoon salt
¼ teaspoon black pepper
  1 tablespoon honey

1. Preheat oven to 425°F. Trim carrots, reserving tops if desired. If desired, peel carrots then cut large carrots lengthwise.

2. Line a shallow roasting pan with parchment paper. Evenly spread carrots in the prepared roasting pan. Drizzle with olive oil. Roast carrots, uncovered, for 20 minutes.

3. Meanwhile, heat a dry small skillet over medium-high heat. Add hazelnuts; cook and stir about 3 minutes or until fragrant and toasted. Transfer to a bowl. Add coriander seeds, sesame seeds, and cumin seeds to hot skillet. Cook over medium-high heat about 2 minutes or until fragrant and toasted. Remove spices from heat and transfer to another bowl to cool.

4. Using a spice grinder, coffee grinder, or mortar and pestle, grind or crush toasted spices just until coarsely ground or desired consistency. Add the hazelnuts, salt, and pepper, crushing nuts slightly. Remove carrots from the oven. Drizzle with honey; toss to evenly coat. Sprinkle carrots with half of the hazelnut mixture. Roast for 5 to 10 minutes more or until carrots are tender.

5. To serve, transfer carrots to a serving platter. Sprinkle with a little more hazelnut-seed mixture and, if desired, drizzle with additional honey.

PER SERVING *152 cal., 9 g fat (1 g sat. fat), 0 mg chol., 274 mg sodium, 17 g carb., 5 g fiber, 3 g pro.*

SPICE-AND-HONEY
ROASTED CARROTS

ROASTED
POTATOES AND
LEEKS

Roasted Potatoes and Leeks

PREP **15 minutes**
ROAST **35 minutes at 425°F**
MAKES **4 servings**

    Nonstick cooking spray
12 ounces tiny new potatoes, scrubbed and quartered
1 tablespoon olive oil
¼ teaspoon salt
⅛ teaspoon black pepper
1 medium red sweet pepper, cut into bite-size strips
1 medium leek, trimmed and cut into ¼-inch-thick slices (white part only)

1. Preheat oven to 425°F. Coat a 13×9×2-inch baking pan with cooking spray; add potatoes to pan. Drizzle with oil and sprinkle with salt and black pepper; toss to coat.
2. Roast, uncovered, for 25 minutes, stirring once. Add sweet pepper and leek; toss to combine. Roast for 10 minutes or just until potatoes are tender and browned on the edges and pepper pieces are tender.
PER SERVING *112 cal., 4 g fat (1 g sat. fat), 0 mg chol., 166 mg sodium, 19 g carb., 2 g fiber, 2 g pro.*

Savory Collard Greens

PREP **1 hour** COOK **20 minutes**
MAKES **8 servings**

5 pounds collard greens (about 6 bunches), cleaned
½ pound pancetta, cut into ½-inch pieces
12 cloves garlic, coarsely chopped
½ teaspoon crushed red pepper
2 cups chicken broth
¼ cup balsamic vinegar
    Salt and black pepper
    Crushed red pepper (optional)

1. Fold each collard green leaf in half lengthwise along the stem. Slice away the tough center stem. Stack the leaves, roll tightly, slice into ½-inch ribbons (about 40 cups). Transfer to a resealable plastic bag and refrigerate up to 3 days.

2. In a 6-to 8-quart stockpot cook pancetta over medium heat for 8 minutes or until crisp and browned. Remove cooked pancetta with a slotted spoon; drain pancetta on paper towels. Add garlic and ½ teaspoon crushed red pepper to drippings in pot; cook for 2 minutes.
3. Add about half the sliced collard greens to stockpot. Pour in chicken broth and vinegar. Cover and cook 5 minutes or until collards cook down.

Add remaining collard greens. Cover and bring to boiling. Reduce heat and simmer on low for 20 to 30 minutes or until greens are tender, stirring occasionally. Season to taste with salt and black pepper. Top with cooked pancetta and, if desired, additional crushed red pepper.
PER SERVING *159 cal., 9 g fat (3 g sat. fat), 11 mg chol., 552 mg sodium, 12 g carb., 7 g fiber, 11 g pro.*

SAVORY COLLARD GREENS

ROASTED CAULIFLOWER SOUP

Roasted Mushroom Soup with Dill and Lemon Gremolata

PREP 30 minutes
ROAST 45 minutes at 400°F
MAKES 4 servings

 8 ounces fresh baby portobello mushrooms, halved
 4 ounces fresh shiitake mushrooms, stemmed and halved
 2 tablespoons olive oil
 ¼ teaspoon salt
 ¼ teaspoon black pepper
1½ cups reduced-sodium chicken broth
 1 tablespoon butter
 ½ cup chopped onion
 2 cloves garlic, minced
 2 tablespoons dry sherry or dry white wine
 4 teaspoons all-purpose flour
 1 cup evaporated fat-free milk
 1 tablespoon snipped fresh dill
1½ teaspoons lemon zest

1. Preheat oven to 400°F. In a 15×10×1-inch baking pan combine portobello and shiitake mushrooms. Drizzle with oil and sprinkle with salt and pepper; toss to coat. Spread mushrooms in a single layer. Roast, covered, for 30 minutes. Roast, uncovered, for 15 to 18 minutes or until mushrooms are tender, yet moist.
2. In a food processor or blender combine half of the mushrooms and ¾ cup of the broth. Cover and process until smooth.
3. In a medium saucepan melt butter over medium heat. Add onion and garlic; cook 5 minutes or until onion is tender, stirring occasionally. Add sherry. Simmer, uncovered, for 1 minute or until most of the liquid is evaporated. Stir in flour; cook for 1 minute. Stir in remaining mushroom halves, pureed mushrooms, remaining broth, and evaporated milk. Bring to boiling; reduce heat. Simmer, uncovered, for 10 minutes or until slightly thickened.
4. For Lemon Gremolata, in a small bowl combine dill and lemon zest. Sprinkle over servings of soup.
PER SERVING 194 cal., 10 g fat (3 g sat. fat), 10 mg chol., 459 mg sodium, 17 g carb., 2 g fiber, 9 g pro.

Roasted Cauliflower Soup

PREP 15 minutes
ROAST 30 minutes at 400°F
COOK 20 minutes MAKES 8 servings

 1 large head cauliflower, cut into florets (10 cups)
 1 onion, sliced
 2 cloves garlic, halved
 2 tablespoons olive oil
 2 14.5-ounce cans chicken broth
 1 cup water
 1 bay leaf
 1 teaspoon snipped fresh thyme or ¼ teaspoon dried thyme, crushed
 1 cup half-and-half or light cream
 1 teaspoon salt
 ⅛ teaspoon black pepper
    Freshly ground black pepper (optional)
    Fresh thyme leaves (optional)

1. Preheat oven to 400°F. In a large roasting pan combine cauliflower, onion, and garlic. Drizzle with oil; toss gently to coat. Spread vegetables in an even layer. Roast, uncovered, for 30 minutes, stirring once.
2. In a 4-quart Dutch oven combine roasted vegetables, broth, the water, bay leaf, and thyme. Bring to boiling; reduce heat. Simmer, covered, for 20 minutes; cool slightly. Remove and discard bay leaf.
3. Transfer vegetable mixture in batches to a food processor or blender. Cover and process or blend until smooth. Return puree to Dutch oven. Stir in half-and-half, salt, and the ⅛ teaspoon pepper. Heat through (do not boil). If desired, sprinkle with pepper and thyme leaves.
PER SERVING 125 cal., 7 g fat (3 g sat. fat), 12 mg chol., 756 mg sodium, 13 g carb., 3 g fiber, 4 g pro.

ROASTED MUSHROOM
SOUP WITH DILL AND
LEMON GREMOLATA

SHRIMP CORN FRITTERS
WITH RED PEPPER SAUCE,
PAGE 36

Small Bites

A SELECTION OF SAVORY appetizers perfectly portioned for sampling is the best kind of party food. These dips, meatballs, wings, crispy corn cakes, stuffed mushrooms, and other nibbles are terrific alone as starters or as part of an appetizer buffet.

APRICOT-CURRY
MEATBALLS

Apricot-Curry Meatballs

PREP 35 minutes
BAKE 25 minutes at 375°F
MAKES 6 servings

- 2 eggs
- ½ cup fine dry bread crumbs
- ½ cup finely chopped onion
- ¼ cup milk
- ½ teaspoon salt
- ½ teaspoon black pepper
- 1 pound ground beef
- 1 pound ground pork
- 1 12-ounce jar apricot preserves
- ⅓ cup soy sauce
- ¼ cup cider vinegar
- 4 teaspoons grated fresh ginger
- 2 teaspoons curry powder

1. Preheat oven to 375°F. In a large bowl beat eggs with a fork. Stir in bread crumbs, onion, milk, salt, and pepper. Add beef and pork; mix well. Shape mixture into 36 meatballs. Place meatballs in a shallow baking pan. Bake for 25 to 30 minutes or until meatballs are cooked through (160°F). Drain off fat.
2. Meanwhile, for the sauce, in a bowl stir together the apricot preserves, soy sauce, vinegar, ginger, and curry powder.
3. Serve immediately or place meatballs in a 3½- or 4-quart slow cooker and keep warm, covered, on warm setting or low-heat setting for up to 2 hours. Serve with apricot sauce.
PER SERVING 99 cal., 5 g fat (2 g sat. fat), 28 mg chol., 216 mg sodium, 8 g carb., 0 g fiber, 5 g pro.

Meatballs in Chipotle Sauce

PREP 40 minutes COOK 10 minutes
MAKES 18 servings

- ¼ cup masa harina (corn tortilla flour)
- ¼ cup hot water
- 8 ounces ground pork
- 8 ounces ground beef
- ¼ cup finely chopped onion
- 3 cloves garlic, minced

MEATBALLS IN CHIPOTLE SAUCE

- 1 teaspoon dried oregano, crushed
- ½ teaspoon salt
- ½ teaspoon ground cumin
- ¼ teaspoon ground allspice
- ¼ teaspoon black pepper
- 2 tablespoons vegetable oil
- 1 14.5-ounce can beef broth
- 1 8-ounce can tomato sauce
- 2 tablespoons tomato paste
- 1 canned chipotle chile pepper in adobo sauce, seeded and finely chopped (tip, page 13)

1. In a large bowl combine masa harina and the hot water. Add pork, beef, onion, garlic, oregano, salt, cumin, allspice, and pepper; mix well. Using moistened hands, shape mixture into 1½-inch meatballs.
2. In a large skillet heat oil over medium heat. Add meatballs; cook until evenly browned and cooked through, stirring frequently.
3. Meanwhile, for sauce, in a medium saucepan combine broth, tomato sauce, tomato paste, and chipotle pepper. Bring to boiling; reduce heat. Simmer, uncovered, for 10 to 15 minutes or until sauce is slightly thickened to desired consistency. Transfer meatballs to a shallow serving dish and pour sauce over meatballs.
PER SERVING 93 cal., 7 g fat (2 g sat. fat), 18 mg chol., 246 mg sodium, 3 g carb., 1 g fiber, 5 g pro.

Ham and Cheddar Sliders with Pineapple-Apricot Jam

PREP 15 minutes
BAKE 20 minutes at 350°F
MAKES 24 servings

¼ cup butter, melted
2 tablespoons all-purpose flour
1 cup pineapple-apricot jam, pineapple jam, or apricot jam
24 dinner rolls
   Nonstick cooking spray
1½ pounds very thinly sliced cooked ham
12 ounces cheddar cheese, thinly sliced
½ cup butter
¼ cup packed brown sugar
4 teaspoons yellow mustard
2 teaspoons Worcestershire sauce
1 to 1½ teaspoons poppy seeds

1. Lightly coat two 13×9×2-inch baking pans with nonstick cooking spray; set aside. In a small bowl combine ¼ cup melted butter, the flour, and the jam, breaking any large pieces of fruit.
2. Cut rolls in half horizontally. Lay roll bottoms, cut sides up, in an even layer in prepared pans. Spread each roll bottom with 1 teaspoon of jam mixture; top with ham and cheese. Add roll tops*.
3. For topping, in a small saucepan melt the ½ cup butter over medium heat. Remove from heat; stir in brown sugar, mustard, and Worcestershire sauce. Using a pastry brush, coat roll tops with topping. Sprinkle roll tops with poppy seeds.
4. Bake sliders in a 350°F oven for 20 minutes or until cheese is melted and sliders are heated through.
PER SERVING *274 cal., 13 g fat (7 g sat. fat), 45 mg chol., 655 mg sodium, 27 g carb., 1 g fiber, 12 g pro.*
*Make Ahead Assemble sliders through Step 2. Cover tightly with plastic wrap; refrigerate up to 24 hours. Just before baking, proceed with Step 3.

Gingery Apricot-Glazed Pork Ribs

PREP 35 minutes
MARINATE 6 hours
BAKE 1 hour 15 minutes at 350°F
MAKES 14 servings

4 pounds pork loin back ribs, halved across the bones*

1 cup finely chopped onion
⅔ cup dry sherry
½ cup rice vinegar
½ cup soy sauce
¼ cup finely chopped fresh ginger
2 tablespoons finely chopped garlic (about 12 cloves)
1 teaspoon black pepper
⅔ cup apricot preserves
3 tablespoons spicy brown mustard
1 tablespoon toasted sesame oil
¼ teaspoon cayenne pepper
1 tablespoon sesame seeds, toasted*
   Sliced green onions (optional)

1. Trim fat from ribs. Cut ribs into single-rib portions. Place rib pieces in a large resealable plastic bag set in a shallow dish. For marinade, in a medium bowl combine onion, sherry, vinegar, soy sauce, ginger, garlic, and black pepper. Pour over ribs; seal bag and turn to coat ribs. Marinate in the refrigerator for 6 to 24 hours, turning bag occasionally.
2. Preheat oven to 350°F. Drain rib pieces, reserving ¼ cup of the marinade. Arrange rib pieces, meaty sides up, in a shallow roasting pan. Roast, uncovered, about 1 hour or until tender.
3. Meanwhile, in a small saucepan combine apricot preserves, mustard, oil, and cayenne pepper. Add the reserved marinade. Bring to boiling; reduce heat. Simmer, uncovered, for 3 minutes.
4. Brush ribs generously with sauce. Bake, uncovered, for 15 minutes, brushing once or twice with sauce during baking. Sprinkle with sesame seeds before serving. If desired, sprinkle with green onions and serve with remaining sauce.
PER SERVING *292 cal., 20 g fat (7 g sat. fat), 65 mg chol., 262 mg sodium, 12 g carb., 0 g fiber, 13 g pro.*
*Tip To toast whole nuts or coconut, spread them in a shallow pan. Bake in a 350°F oven for 5 to 10 minutes, shaking the pan once or twice and watching closely to avoid burning. Toast finely chopped or ground nuts or seeds in a dry skillet over medium heat. Stir often to prevent burning.

HAM AND CHEDDAR SLIDERS WITH PINEAPPLE-APRICOT JAM

GINGERY APRICOT-
GLAZED PORK RIBS

CHIPOTLE-CHICKEN
AND BLACK BEAN
NACHOS

Chipotle-Chicken and Black Bean Nachos

PREP 30 minutes
SLOW COOK 5 hours (low) or
2½ hours (high)
MAKES 12 servings

- 1 tablespoon chili powder
- 2 teaspoons onion powder
- 1 teaspoon ground cumin
- 1 teaspoon garlic powder
- 1 teaspoon smoked paprika
- ½ teaspoon salt
- 2 pounds skinless, boneless chicken thighs
- 2 10-ounce cans diced tomatoes with green chile peppers, undrained
- 1 15-ounce can black beans, rinsed and drained
- 2 tablespoons lime juice
- 1 tablespoon finely chopped canned chipotle chile peppers in adobo sauce (tip, page 13)
- 1 10-ounce package large tortilla chips
- 1½ cups shredded Mexican-style four-cheese blend (6 ounces)
- ¼ cup sliced green onions
- ¼ cup sliced or halved pimiento-stuffed green olives
- 2 tablespoons snipped fresh cilantro
- ¾ cup sour cream
- ¾ cup fresh tomato salsa

1. In a small bowl combine chili powder, onion powder, cumin, garlic powder, smoked paprika, and salt. Sprinkle seasoning over chicken; rub in with your fingers. Place chicken in a 3½- or 4-quart slow cooker.
2. In a medium bowl combine tomatoes with green chile peppers, black beans, lime juice, and chipotle peppers. Pour over chicken in cooker.
3. Cover and cook on low-heat setting for 5 to 6 hours or high-heat setting for 2½ to 3 hours. Remove chicken from cooker. Using a potato masher, mash beans in cooker. Shred or chop chicken; return to cooker.
4. Preheat oven to 375°F. Arrange tortilla chips on a large oven-safe serving platter. Using a slotted spoon, scoop Chipotle-Chicken on chips. Sprinkle with cheese; bake for 5 minutes or until is cheese melted.

Remove from oven and sprinkle with green onions, olives, and cilantro. Serve with sour cream and salsa.
PER SERVING *331 cal., 16 g fat (6 g sat. fat), 81 mg chol., 816 mg sodium, 26 g carb., 4 g fiber, 23 g pro.*

Thai Chicken Wings with Peanut Sauce

PREP 25 minutes
SLOW COOK 5 hours (low) or
2½ hours (high)   MAKES 12 servings

- 24 chicken wing drummettes (about 2¼ pounds total)
- ½ cup salsa
- 2 tablespoons creamy peanut butter
- 1 tablespoon lime juice
- 2 teaspoons soy sauce
- 2 teaspoons grated fresh ginger
- ¼ cup sugar
- ¼ cup creamy peanut butter
- 3 tablespoons soy sauce
- 3 tablespoons water
- 2 cloves garlic, minced

1. Place chicken drummettes in a 3½- or 4-quart slow cooker. In a bowl combine salsa, 2 tablespoons peanut butter, lime juice, 2 teaspoons soy sauce, and ginger. Pour over chicken; toss to coat.
2. Cover and cook on low-heat setting for 5 to 6 hours or high-heat setting for 2½ to 3 hours.
3. Meanwhile, for Peanut Sauce, in a small saucepan combine sugar, ¼ cup peanut butter, 3 tablespoons soy sauce, the water, and garlic. Stir over medium-low heat until sugar is dissolved and sauce is smooth. Set aside (sauce will thicken as it cools).
4. Drain chicken, discarding cooking liquid. Return chicken to cooker. Gently stir in peanut sauce. Serve immediately or keep warm, covered, on warm- or low-heat setting up to 2 hours.
PER SERVING *189 cal., 13 g fat (3 g sat. fat), 58 mg chol., 392 mg sodium, 6 g carb., 1 g fiber, 12 g pro.*

THAI CHICKEN WINGS WITH PEANUT SAUCE

PROSCIUTTO-WRAPPED
ASPARAGUS

Prosciutto-Wrapped Asparagus

START TO FINISH 20 minutes
MAKES 8 servings

24 asparagus spears (1 to
    1¼ pounds), trimmed to about
    6-inch lengths
24 thin slices provolone cheese
    (12 to 14 ounces)
12 paper-thin slices prosciutto,
    halved lengthwise (8 to
    10 ounces)
 1 to 2 tablespoons olive oil
 1 to 2 tablespoons balsamic vinegar
    Cracked black pepper

1. Place a steamer basket in a large
skillet. Add water to just below bottom
of basket. Bring to boiling. Place
asparagus in basket. Reduce heat to
medium-low. Steam, covered, for
4 minutes. Remove asparagus from
basket; immerse in ice water to cool
quickly. Drain asparagus; pat dry with
paper towels.
2. Wrap a slice of cheese and a
half-slice of prosciutto around each
asparagus spear. Arrange wrapped
asparagus on a serving plate.
3. Before serving, drizzle with oil and
balsamic vinegar and sprinkle with
cracked pepper.
PER SERVING *268 cal., 20 g fat
(8 g sat. fat), 29 mg chol., 876 mg sodium,
4 g carb., 1 g fiber, 19 g pro.*

Shrimp Corn Fritters with Red Pepper Sauce

(photo on page 28)

START TO FINISH 40 minutes
MAKES 8 servings

 2 lemons
 1 pound fresh or frozen peeled,
    deveined medium shrimp
 3 ears fresh sweet corn, kernels
    removed (1½ cups)
 3 green onions, thinly sliced
 2 tablespoons snipped fresh Italian
    parsley
 1 jalapeño, minced (tip, page 13)
 1 teaspoon salt
 8 ounces Greek-style yogurt
 4 ounces roasted red sweet
    peppers, drained

FOUR-CHEESE
STUFFED
MUSHROOMS

1 tablespoon minced fresno chile
   pepper (tip, page 13)
1 tablespoon fresh lemon juice
1 clove garlic
1 teaspoon honey (optional)
   Kosher salt to taste
½ cup vegetable oil
   Snipped fresh Italian parsley
   (optional)

1. Remove zest from lemons.
2. For Shrimp Corn Fritters, place
about two-thirds of the shrimp and
half the lemon zest in a food processor.
Cover and process until the mixture
becomes a paste. Transfer to a bowl.
3. Roughly chop remaining shrimp;
add to shrimp paste. Add remaining
lemon zest, corn kernels, green onions,
parsley, jalapeño, and salt; mix well.
Shape into eight patties. Cover and
chill until ready to use.
4. For Red Pepper Sauce, in a blender
or food processor, blend the yogurt,
roasted red peppers, minced chile
pepper, lemon juice, garlic, honey (if
using), and salt. Cover and chill until
ready to use.
5. In a large skillet heat oil over
medium-high heat. Working in two
batches cook half the fritters for 2 to
3 minutes or until the bottoms are

golden and crispy. Turn fritters and
cook 1 to 2 minutes or until golden and
shrimp is opaque. Remove from heat;
cover and keep warm while cooking
remaining fritters.
6. If desired, sprinkle with parsley and
serve with Red Pepper Sauce.
PER SERVING *219 cal., 14 g fat
(2 g sat. fat), 92 mg chol., 436 mg sodium,
9 g carb., 1 g fiber, 16 g pro.*

Four-Cheese Stuffed Mushrooms

PREP **20 minutes**
BAKE **12 minutes at 350°F/8 minutes
at 450°F** MAKES **8 servings**

24 large fresh mushrooms (1½ to
    2 inches in diameter)
1   tablespoon olive oil
8   dried tomatoes (not oil-pack)
    Boiling water
1   cup light ricotta cheese
½   cup finely chopped fresh spinach
½   cup shredded reduced-fat
    Monterey Jack cheese (2 ounces)
3   tablespoons freshly grated
    Parmesan cheese
1   tablespoon snipped fresh basil
2   cloves garlic, minced
¼   teaspoon salt

¼   teaspoon black pepper
½   cup crumbled reduced-fat feta
    cheese (2 ounces)

1. Preheat oven to 350°F. Remove and
discard mushroom stems. In a medium
to large bowl toss mushroom caps
with oil to coat. Arrange in a shallow
baking pan, stem sides down. Bake for
12 minutes; drain off liquid. Increase
oven temperature to 450°F.
2. Meanwhile, for filling, in a small
bowl pour enough boiling water over
dried tomatoes to cover; let stand
10 minutes. Drain tomatoes; discard
liquid. Coarsely snip tomatoes and
place in a medium bowl. Add ricotta
cheese, spinach, Monterey Jack cheese,
Parmesan cheese, basil, garlic, salt,
and pepper. Turn mushroom caps
stem sides up; fill caps with filling.
Sprinkle with feta cheese.
3. Bake for 8 to 10 minutes or until
heated through and lightly browned.
PER SERVING *115 cal., 7 g fat
(3 g sat. fat), 19 mg chol., 285 mg sodium,
6 g carb., 1 g fiber, 9 g pro.*

CREAMY CRAB
RANGOON DIP WITH
WONTON CHIPS

Creamy Crab Rangoon Dip with Wonton Chips

PREP 20 minutes
BAKE 5 minutes at 375°F
CHILL 2 hours MAKES 10 servings

20 wonton wrappers
    Nonstick cooking spray
1 8-ounce tub light cream cheese
   spread
¼ cup sour cream
1 8-ounce package flake-style
   imitation crabmeat, chopped
½ cup finely chopped water
   chestnuts (optional)
¼ cup finely chopped green onion
1 tablespoon powdered sugar
½ teaspoon lemon juice
½ teaspoon reduced-sodium soy
   sauce
1 clove garlic, minced
   Bottled sweet-and-sour sauce
   Thinly bias-sliced green onions

1. Preheat oven to 375°F. For wonton chips, use a sharp knife to cut wonton wrappers diagonally in half to form 40 triangles. Arrange triangles in a single layer on baking sheets. Lightly spray with cooking spray, carefully turn, and spray again. Bake for 5 minutes or until edges are golden brown. Set aside or store in an airtight container up to 2 days.
2. For the dip, in a medium bowl stir together cream cheese and sour cream. Add crab, water chestnuts (if using), ¼ cup green onion, the powdered sugar, lemon juice, soy sauce, and garlic; stir well. Cover and chill for 2 to 24 hours. (To serve dip warm, place in a microwave-safe bowl and heat 1 to 2 minutes on high, stirring every 30 seconds.)
3. To serve, drizzle cold or warm dip with sweet-and-sour sauce then sprinkle with green onions.
PER SERVING *141 cal., 6 g fat (3 g sat. fat), 23 mg chol., 405 mg sodium, 16 g carb., 1 g fiber, 5 g pro.*

Asiago-Artichoke Dip

PREP 20 minutes
BAKE 30 minutes at 350°F
COOL 15 minutes
MAKES 12 servings

ASIAGO-ARTICHOKE DIP

1 14-ounce can artichoke hearts,
   rinsed and drained
2 ounces thinly sliced prosciutto
   or 2 slices bacon
1 cup arugula or fresh spinach,
   chopped
1 8-ounce carton sour cream
3 tablespoons all-purpose flour
½ cup mayonnaise
½ cup bottled roasted red sweet
   peppers, drained and finely
   chopped
¾ cup finely shredded Asiago
   cheese or Parmesan cheese
   (3 ounces)
¼ cup thinly sliced green onions
   Chopped and crisp-cooked
   prosciutto or bacon (optional)
   Assorted crackers, pita chips,
   and/or toasted baguette slices

1. Preheat oven to 350°F. Place artichoke hearts in a fine-mesh sieve. To remove excess liquid, firmly press on artichoke hearts with paper towels. Chop artichoke hearts; set aside.
2. Stack the 2 ounces prosciutto; snip or cut crosswise into thin strips. Separate pieces as much as possible. In a medium skillet brown prosciutto over medium heat until slightly crisp. Add arugula; cook for 1 minute.
3. In a large bowl stir together sour cream and flour until combined. Stir in mayonnaise and roasted peppers, ½ cup of the cheese, the green onions, artichokes, and arugula mixture. Transfer to an ungreased 9-inch pie plate. Sprinkle with the remaining ¼ cup cheese (if desired, set aside 1 tablespoon cheese to sprinkle before serving).

4. Bake, uncovered, for 30 minutes or until edges are lightly browned and dip is hot in center. Cool for 15 minutes before serving. If desired, sprinkle with additional prosciutto and reserved cheese. Serve with crackers, pita chips, and/or baguette slices.
PER SERVING *157 cal., 14 g fat (5 g sat. fat), 26 mg chol., 324 mg sodium, 4 g carb., 1 g fiber, 4 g pro.*

Rosemary Roasted Nuts

PREP 15 minutes
BAKE 12 minutes at 375°F
MAKES 30 servings

3 cups whole unblanched almonds
1½ cups walnuts
1 cup raw pumpkin seeds (pepitas)
2 tablespoons finely snipped fresh
   rosemary
2 teaspoons packed brown sugar
1 teaspoon sea salt
½ teaspoon cayenne pepper
2 tablespoons butter, melted

1. Preheat oven to 375°F. In a 15×10×1-inch baking pan combine almonds, walnuts, and pumpkin seeds. Bake for 12 minutes or until toasted, stirring once.
2. In a small bowl combine rosemary, brown sugar, salt, and cayenne pepper. Stir in butter. Drizzle butter mixture over nuts; toss gently to coat. Serve warm or at room temperature. Store in an airtight container up to 3 days.
PER SERVING *177 cal., 15 g fat (2 g sat. fat), 2 mg chol., 60 mg sodium, 5 g carb., 2 g fiber, 6 g pro.*

Gingered Citrus Fizz

START TO FINISH **10 minutes**
MAKES **4 servings**

- 3 medium oranges
- 3 medium limes
- 1 1-inch piece fresh ginger, peeled and thinly sliced
  Ice
- 3 cups ginger ale

1. Using a vegetable peeler, remove the peel from the oranges in 12 long strips and from the limes in 12 long strips, avoiding the pith. Cut oranges and limes in half. Juice enough of the orange and lime halves to get ¾ cup orange juice and ¼ cup lime juice. (Reserve remaining orange and lime halves for another use.) In a glass measure combine orange juice and lime juice.
2. Fill four 16-ounce glasses halfway with ice. Evenly divide orange peel strips, lime peel strips, and ginger slices among the glasses. Fill glasses with more ice. Evenly divide juice mixture among glasses. Slowly add ginger ale. Serve immediately.
PER SERVING *87 cal., 0 g fat, 0 mg chol., 14 mg sodium, 22 g carb., 0 g fiber, 0 g pro.*

Glogg

PREP **20 minutes**
SLOW COOK **5 hours (low)**
MAKES **16 servings**

- 2 tangerines
- 4 4-inch sticks cinnamon
- 10 ¼-inch-thick slices fresh ginger, unpeeled
- 12 whole cloves
- 10 whole cardamom pods
- 2 750-milliliter bottles Merlot or dry red wine
- 2 cups port
- 1 cup sugar
- 1 cup vodka
- 1 cup chopped dried figs
- 1 cup dried cranberries
  Additional cinnamon sticks

1. With a paring knife or vegetable peeler remove the peels from tangerines in strips; set aside. Wrap fruit in plastic wrap; chill until needed. For spice bag, cut an 8-inch square from a double thickness of 100%-cotton cheesecloth. Place tangerine peel, the 4 cinnamon sticks, the ginger, cloves, and cardamom pods in the center of cheesecloth. Bring up corners of the cheesecloth; tie bag closed with 100%-cotton string.
2. In a 6-quart slow cooker combine spice bag, Merlot, port, sugar, vodka, figs, and cranberries.
3. Cover and cook on low-heat setting for 5 to 6 hours. Discard spice bag. Just before serving, slice tangerines then add to glogg in cooker.
4. Ladle glogg into mugs. Serve with an additional cinnamon stick.
PER SERVING *258 cal., 0 g fat, 0 mg chol., 6 mg sodium, 33 g carb., 2 g fiber, 1 g pro.*

Silky Raspberry Hot Chocolate

PREP **10 minutes**
SLOW COOK **5 hours (low) or 2½ hours (high)**
MAKES **12 servings**

- 4 cups half-and-half or light cream
- 4 cups whole milk
- 1 12-ounce package bittersweet chocolate pieces (2 cups) or 12 ounces bittersweet chocolate, chopped
- ½ cup milk chocolate pieces
- ½ cup raspberry liqueur or raspberry beverage flavoring syrup
- 1 tablespoon vanilla
- 1 recipe Chocolate-Hazelnut Cream (optional)
  Grated bittersweet chocolate (optional)

1. In a 3½- or 4-quart slow cooker stir together half-and-half and milk.
2. Cover and cook on low-heat setting for 5 to 6 hours or on high-heat setting for 2½ to 3 hours.
3. If necessary, skim "skin" from surface; discard. Stir in bittersweet chocolate pieces and milk chocolate pieces. Whisk until chocolate is melted and mixture is smooth. Serve immediately or keep warm, covered, on warm or low-heat setting up to 2 hours.
4. Just before serving, stir in raspberry liqueur and vanilla. Ladle into mugs. If desired, top each serving with Chocolate-Hazelnut Cream and grated chocolate.
PER SERVING *464 cal., 34 g fat (20 g sat. fat), 68 mg chol., 83 mg sodium, 35 g carb., 3 g fiber, 8 g pro.*

Chocolate-Hazelnut Cream In a medium mixing bowl beat 1 cup whipping cream, 2 tablespoons chocolate-hazelnut spread, and 2 teaspoons sugar with a mixer on medium until soft peaks form (tips curl). (The cream may take longer to whip because of the chocolate-hazelnut spread.) Makes about 2 cups.

GINGERED CITRUS FIZZ

SILKY RASPBERRY
HOT CHOCOLATE

SMOKED SALMON
EGGS BENEDICT,
PAGE 46

In the Morning

ROUSE SLEEPYHEADS from their slumber with
breakfast and brunch dishes that suit every taste
and occasion. Choose from a selection of savory egg
dishes and stuffed crepes as well as sweets such
as cinnamon rolls, oven-baked French toast,
or flaky breakfast tarts.

BREAKFAST TARTS,
PAGE 53

SPANISH-STYLE
STRATA

Spanish-Style Strata

PREP 40 minutes
CHILL 1 hour
BAKE 55 minutes at 325°F
STAND 10 minutes
MAKES 8 servings

Nonstick cooking spray
7 cups 1-inch cubes crusty
   country bread
16 ounces cooked chicken sausage
   links, cut into ½-inch pieces
1 14.5-ounce can diced tomatoes
   with Italian herbs, drained
¼ cup chopped roasted red sweet
   peppers, drained
¼ cup sliced green onions
¼ cup sliced pitted green olives
1 cup shredded Manchego cheese
6 eggs, beaten
3 cups milk
½ teaspoon paprika
½ teaspoon dried oregano, crushed
½ teaspoon black pepper
   Snipped fresh Italian parsley
   (optional)

1. Lightly coat a 13×9×2-inch baking
dish with cooking spray. Spread half
the bread cubes in the dish. In a large
bowl combine the sausage pieces,
tomatoes, roasted sweet peppers,
green onions, and olives. Spoon half
the sausage mixture over bread cubes.
Sprinkle with half the cheese. Top with
the remaining bread cubes, sausage
mixture, and cheese.
2. In a large bowl whisk together eggs,
milk, paprika, oregano, and black
pepper. Evenly pour over strata. Cover
and chill for 1 to 24 hours.
3. Preheat oven to 325°F. Bake,
covered, for 30 minutes. Uncover
and bake for 25 to 30 minutes more
or until the internal temperature
registers 170°F on an instant-read
thermometer. Let stand for 10 minutes
before serving. If desired, sprinkle
with parsley.
PER SERVING *362 cal., 13 g fat
(6 g sat. fat), 223 mg chol., 1,183 mg sodium,
33 g carb., 2 g fiber, 26 g pro.*

BREAKFAST HAM
AND EGG CUPS

Breakfast Ham and Egg Cups

PREP 20 minutes
BAKE 18 minutes at 350°F
STAND 3 minutes MAKES 8 servings

Nonstick cooking spray
8 thin slices deli-style cooked ham
¼ cup shredded Italian cheese blend
   or mozzarella cheese (1 ounce)
8 eggs
   Black pepper
8 teaspoons basil pesto (optional)
8 cherry tomatoes or grape
   tomatoes, halved

1. Preheat oven to 350°F. Coat eight
2½-inch muffin cups with cooking
spray. Gently press a ham slice onto
the bottom and up the sides of each
prepared muffin cup, carefully ruffling
the edges of ham. Divide cheese among
the ham-lined muffin cups.
2. One at a time, break an egg into a
measuring cup then slip egg into a
muffin cup. Sprinkle with pepper. If
desired, spoon 1 teaspoon of the pesto
onto each egg. Top with tomato halves.
3. Bake for 18 to 20 minutes or until
whites are completely set and yolks are
thickened. Let stand in muffin cups for
3 to 5 minutes before serving. Carefully
remove ham and egg cups from pan.
PER SERVING *145 cal., 10 g fat
(3 g sat. fat), 202 mg chol., 413 mg sodium,
2 g carb., 1 g fiber, 11 g pro.*

Smoked Salmon Eggs Benedict

(photo on page 42)

START TO FINISH **25 minutes**
MAKES **4 servings**

¼ cup light sour cream
1 teaspoon lemon juice
¾ to 1 teaspoon yellow mustard
3 to 4 teaspoons fat-free milk
8 eggs
4 whole wheat English muffins, split and toasted
4 ounces thinly sliced smoked salmon (lox-style)
    Snipped fresh chives (optional)
    Paprika (optional)

1. For sauce, in a small bowl combine sour cream, lemon juice, and mustard. Stir in enough of the milk to reach desired consistency. Set aside.
2. Lightly grease four cups of an egg poaching pan.* Place poacher cups over the pan of boiling water (water should not touch bottoms of cups); reduce heat to simmering. Break each egg into a cup then slip egg into a poacher cup. Cook, covered, for 4 to 6 minutes or until whites are completely set and yolks begin to thicken but are not hard. Run a knife around edges to loosen eggs. Invert poacher cups to transfer eggs to a large pan of warm water to keep them warm. Repeat with the remaining four eggs.

3. To serve, layer muffin halves with smoked salmon and poached eggs. Spoon sauce over eggs. If desired, sprinkle with chives and paprika.
PER SERVING *329 cal., 13 g fat (4 g sat. fat), 383 mg chol., 970 mg sodium, 29 g carb., 4 g fiber, 24 g pro.*
***Tip** If you don't have an egg-poaching pan, lightly grease a large skillet with vegetable oil or shortening. Half fill the skillet with water. Bring to boiling; reduce heat to simmering. One at a time, break four of the eggs into a cup then slip egg into the simmering water, allowing each egg equal amount of space. Simmer, uncovered, for 3 to 5 minutes or until whites are completely set and yolks begin to thicken but are not hard. Using a slotted spoon, transfer eggs to a large pan of warm water to keep warm. Repeat with the remaining eggs.

Chicken and Spinach Crepes with Mushroom Cream Sauce

PREP **40 minutes**
BAKE **20 minutes at 375°F**
MAKES **8 servings**

1 recipe Crepes or 20 purchased ready-to-use crepes
1 tablespoon butter
1 5-ounce package fresh spinach
1½ cups shredded cooked chicken
½ of an 8-ounce can sliced water chestnuts, drained and coarsely chopped
½ cup shredded part-skim mozzarella cheese (2 ounces)
½ cup low-fat cottage cheese
¼ cup finely shredded Parmesan cheese (1 ounce)
½ teaspoon salt
⅛ teaspoon ground nutmeg
⅛ teaspoon black pepper
    Nonstick cooking spray
2 tablespoons butter
½ cup finely chopped onion
1 pound fresh button or cremini mushrooms, sliced
½ cup chicken or beef broth
½ teaspoon instant chicken or beef bouillon granules
1½ cups whipping cream

2 tablespoons dry Marsala or dry sherry
    Snipped fresh Italian parsley (optional)

1. Prepare Crepes; set aside. In a large nonstick skillet melt the 1 tablespoon butter over medium-high heat. Add spinach. Toss in skillet for 30 to 60 seconds or just until spinach is wilted. Remove from heat. Transfer to a large bowl. Stir in chicken, water chestnuts, mozzarella cheese, cottage cheese, Parmesan cheese, salt, nutmeg, and pepper.
2. Preheat oven to 375°F. Coat a 3-quart rectangular baking dish with cooking spray.
3. Spread about 2 tablespoons of the chicken-spinach filling over half of each crepe. Fold each crepe in half; fold in half again, forming a triangle. Arrange filled crepes in the baking dish, overlapping slightly.
4. Bake for 20 to 25 minutes or until heated through.
5. For Mushroom Sauce, in a large nonstick skillet melt the 2 tablespoons butter over medium heat. Add onion; cook for 2 minutes. Add mushrooms; cook for 5 minutes more. Add broth and bouillon granules; cook and stir until boiling, scraping up browned bits from the skillet. Stir in whipping cream. Simmer, uncovered, for 10 to 12 minutes or until sauce is thickened and bubbly. Add Marsala; cook and stir for 1 minute more.
6. Serve mushroom sauce over filled crepes. If desired, sprinkle with parsley
Crepes In a blender combine 2 eggs, beaten; 1½ cups milk; 1 cup flour; 1 tablespoon butter; 1 teaspoon sugar; and ¼ teaspoon salt; blend until smooth. Heat a lightly greased 6-inch skillet over medium-high heat; remove from heat. Pour in about 2 tablespoons of the batter; lift and tilt skillet to evenly spread batter. Return to heat; cook for 1 minute or until browned on one side; flip with a spatula and cook 1 minute more. Slide crepe onto paper towel-lined plate. Repeat with remaining batter, greasing skillet occasionally. If crepes brown too quickly, reduce heat to medium.
PER SERVING *440 cal., 30 g fat (16 g sat. fat), 159 mg chol., 593 mg sodium, 21 g carb., 2 g fiber, 22 g pro.*

SMOKED SALMON
EGGS BENEDICT

CHICKEN AND SPINACH
CREPES WITH
MUSHROOM CREAM
SAUCE

POTATO
FRITTATA

Potato Frittata

PREP 25 minutes COOK 10 minutes
BAKE 15 minutes at 375°F
STAND 5 minutes MAKES 6 servings

- 1 pound Yukon gold or russet potatoes, scrubbed and thinly sliced
- 2 tablespoons olive oil
- 1½ cups thinly sliced carrots
- 12 eggs, lightly beaten
- ½ cup chopped green onions
- ½ teaspoon salt
- ¼ teaspoon black pepper
- ½ cup halved yellow cherry tomatoes
- 1 clove garlic, minced
  Snipped fresh parsley and/or cilantro

1. Preheat oven to 375°F. In a large ovenproof nonstick skillet cook potatoes in hot oil over medium heat for 5 minutes. Add carrots; cook for 5 minutes or until potatoes and carrots are tender and lightly browned, stirring occasionally.
2. In a medium bowl whisk together the eggs, half the green onions, the salt, and pepper. Pour egg mixture over potato mixture in skillet. Place skillet in oven. Bake, uncovered, 15 to 18 minutes or until frittata appears dry on top. Remove from oven. Let stand on a wire rack for 5 minutes.
3. Meanwhile, for the tomato relish, in a small bowl gently toss together the remaining green onions, cherry tomatoes, garlic, and parsley. Set aside.
4. With a spatula, loosen edges of frittata from skillet. Cut frittata into wedges. Serve with tomato relish.
PER SERVING *259 cal., 14 g fat (4 g sat. fat), 372 mg chol., 362 mg sodium, 18 g carb., 3 g fiber, 15 g pro.*

HERBED SALAD

Herbed Salad

START TO FINISH 15 minutes
MAKES 6 servings

- 6 to 8 cups mixed baby salad greens
- 1½ cups assorted fresh herbs, such as chives, basil, parsley, and/or mint, torn
- 12 to 16 radishes, thinly sliced
- 1 cup bottled Parmesan salad dressing

1. In a large serving bowl toss together salad greens and herbs. Top with sliced radishes. Pass dressing.
PER SERVING *215 cal., 22 g fat (5 g sat. fat), 7 mg chol., 161 mg sodium, 5 g carb., 1 g fiber, 2 g pro.*

MACERATED GRAPEFRUIT WITH PISTACHIOS AND POMEGRANATE

Macerated Grapefruit with Pistachios and Pomegranate

PREP 25 minutes CHILL 1 hour
MAKES 4 servings

½ cup unsweetened pink grapefruit juice
¼ cup honey
½ teaspoon ground coriander
4 large pink, red, and/or white grapefruits
¼ cup coarsely chopped pistachio nuts, macadamia nuts, or pecans
¼ cup pomegranate seeds, toasted flaked coconut, finely chopped maraschino cherries, plain Greek yogurt, and/or finely shredded orange, lemon, or lime peel

1. In a small bowl combine grapefruit juice, honey, and coriander. Mix well.
2. With a sharp knife, remove skin and white membrane from grapefruits. Slice grapefruits crosswise into ¼-inch-thick rounds. Transfer slices to a large wide-mouth jar; add the grapefruit juice mixture. Cover and chill for at least 1 hour or up to 5 days.
3. To serve, divide grapefruit slices among four shallow bowls; pour liquid over slices then top with nuts and pomegranate seeds.

PER SERVING 250 cal., 4 g fat
(0 g sat. fat), 0 mg chol., 36 mg sodium,
55 g carb., 5 g fiber, 4 g pro.

Grape-Yogurt Breakfast Salad with Candied Walnuts

START TO FINISH 30 minutes
MAKES 6 servings

4 ounces reduced-fat cream cheese (Neufchâtel), softened
1 cup vanilla-flavor low-fat Greek yogurt
¼ cup honey
2 teaspoons finely shredded lemon peel
½ teaspoon vanilla
2 pounds green and/or red seedless grapes, halved (about 5 cups)
1 cup purchased candied walnuts or toasted chopped walnuts (tip, page 32)
1 teaspoon fresh thyme leaves
Honey (optional)

1. In a large bowl beat cream cheese with a mixer on medium to high for 30 seconds. Add yogurt, the ¼ cup honey, the lemon peel, and vanilla. Beat on medium until light and smooth. Add grapes; toss to coat.

2. To serve, sprinkle each serving with candied nuts and fresh thyme leaves. If desired, drizzle with additional honey.
PER SERVING 371 cal., 16 g fat
(5 g sat. fat), 19 mg chol., 102 mg sodium,
53 g carb., 2 g fiber, 9 g pro.

Pistachio-Dried Cranberry Buttermilk Pancakes

START TO FINISH 25 minutes
MAKES 12 servings

1¾ cups all-purpose flour
2 tablespoons sugar
1 tablespoon baking powder
¼ teaspoon salt
1 egg, lightly beaten
1½ cups buttermilk or sour milk*
3 tablespoons vegetable oil
⅓ cup chopped pistachio nuts
⅓ cup dried cranberries
Butter (optional)
Finely chopped pistachio nuts (optional)
Desired syrup (optional)

1. In a large bowl stir together flour, sugar, baking powder, and salt. In a medium bowl combine egg, buttermilk, and oil. Add egg mixture all at once to flour mixture. Stir just until moistened (batter should be slightly lumpy). Stir in the ⅓ cup pistachios and the dried cranberries.
2. For each pancake, pour about ¼ cup batter onto a hot, lightly greased griddle or heavy skillet, spreading batter if necessary. Cook over medium heat for 1 to 2 minutes on each side or until pancakes are golden brown. Turn over when surfaces are bubbly and edges are slightly dry. Serve warm. If desired, top with butter and finely chopped pistachios and serve with syrup.
PER SERVING 154 cal., 6 g fat
(1 g sat. fat), 17 mg chol., 224 mg sodium,
22 g carb., 1 g fiber, 4 g pro.
*Tip To make 1½ cups sour milk, place 4½ teaspoons lemon juice or vinegar in a glass measuring cup. Add enough milk to equal 1½ cups total liquid; stir. Let stand for 5 minutes before using.

PISTACHIO-DRIED
CRANBERRY
BUTTERMILK
PANCAKES

AMARETTO BRIOCHE
BAKE

Amaretto Brioche Bake

PREP 20 minutes CHILL 4 hours
BAKE 40 minutes at 350°F
STAND 15 minutes
MAKES 8 servings

  1 cup packed brown sugar
 ⅓ cup butter or margarine
 ¼ cup amaretto
  2 tablespoons light-color corn
     syrup
  1 12-ounce loaf brioche or other
     sweet bread, cut into 8 slices
  4 eggs, lightly beaten
  2 cups half-and-half, light cream,
     or milk
1½ teaspoons vanilla
 ½ teaspoon salt
 ¼ teaspoon ground nutmeg or
     cardamom
1½ cups blackberries (optional)
  2 tablespoons granulated sugar
     (optional)

1. Lightly grease a 3-quart rectangular
baking dish; set aside. In a medium
saucepan combine brown sugar,
butter, amaretto, and corn syrup.
Cook until mixture comes to boiling.
Boil, uncovered, for 1 minute. Pour
into baking dish. Arrange bread slices
on brown sugar mixture.
2. In a medium bowl combine eggs,
half-and-half, vanilla, salt, and
nutmeg. Evenly pour over bread slices.
Press lightly with a large spoon to
moisten all the bread. Cover and chill
4 to 24 hours.
3. Preheat oven to 350°F. Bake,
uncovered, for 40 to 45 minutes or
until a knife inserted near center
comes out clean and the top is lightly
browned. Let stand 15 minutes.
4. Meanwhile, if desired, in a small
bowl combine blackberries and
granulated sugar; lightly crush berries.
Let stand until syrup forms, stirring
occasionally. To serve, if desired,
spoon berries over bread and/or
sprinkle with powdered sugar.
PER SERVING 470 cal., 23 g fat
(11 g sat. fat), 188 mg chol., 432 mg sodium,
55 g carb., 1 g fiber, 9 g pro.

Breakfast Tarts

PREP 25 minutes
BAKE 17 minutes at 375°F
COOL 5 minutes MAKES 6 servings

1¾ cups all-purpose flour
  1 tablespoon sugar
 ½ teaspoon salt
 ¾ cup butter
  1 egg, lightly beaten
  2 to 4 tablespoons milk
  6 tablespoons strawberry jam
     or jelly
     Milk
  1 recipe Vanilla Icing

1. For pastry, in a large bowl stir
together flour, sugar, and salt. Using
a pastry blender, cut in butter until
pastry resembles fine crumbs. Stir
beaten egg into flour mixture. Using
the 2 to 4 tablespoons milk, sprinkle
1 tablespoon of the milk over part of
the flour mixture; toss gently with a
fork. Push moistened pastry to side
of bowl. Repeat moistening pastry,
using 1 tablespoon milk at a time until
moistened. Gather into a ball; knead
gently until pastry holds together.
Divide pastry in half; form halves into
balls. If desired, cover with plastic
wrap and chill until ready to use.
2. Preheat oven to 375°F. On a lightly
floured surface slightly flatten one
pastry ball. Roll into a 9×8-inch
rectangle, trimming as necessary
to form straight edges. Cut in half
lengthwise to form two 9×4-inch
rectangles; cut each in thirds crosswise
to form three 4×3-inch rectangles.
Repeat with the remaining pastry ball
(twelve 4×3-inch rectangles total).
3. Spoon 1 tablespoon of the jam onto
each of six pastry rectangles; spread to
within ½ inch of edges. Moisten edges
with additional milk and top with the
remaining pastry rectangles; press
edges together with a fork to seal.
Using a floured spatula, transfer filled
pastries to a baking sheet. Brush tops
with additional milk; prick with a fork.
4. Bake for 17 to 20 minutes or until
tarts are golden. Transfer to a wire
rack; cool for 5 minutes. Drizzle with
Vanilla Icing; serve warm.
Vanilla Icing In a small bowl stir
together 1 cup powdered sugar,
1 tablespoon milk, and ¼ teaspoon
vanilla. Stir in additional milk,
1 teaspoon at a time, to reach drizzling
consistency.
PER SERVING 496 cal., 24 g fat
(15 g sat. fat), 93 mg chol., 421 mg sodium,
64 g carb., 1 g fiber, 5 g pro.

BREAKFAST TARTS

Nutty Honey Mini Rolls

PREP 25 minutes
BAKE 10 minutes at 375°F
MAKES 24 servings

Nonstick cooking spray
¼ cup finely chopped toasted almonds
2 tablespoons butter, softened
2 tablespoons honey
1 teaspoon ground cinnamon
1 8-ounce package refrigerated crescent dough for recipes or refrigerated crescent rolls
1 recipe Honey Icing

1. Preheat oven to 375°F. Lightly coat twenty-four 1¾-inch muffin cups with cooking spray; set aside. Reserve half the almonds. For filling, in a small bowl stir together the remaining almonds, the butter, honey, and cinnamon; set aside.
2. Unroll crescent dough and cut into two equal rectangles; or, if using regular crescent roll dough, pinch together seams of dough pieces to form two equal rectangles.

3. Spread filling over dough rectangles, leaving about ¼ inch unfilled along long sides. Starting from a long side, roll up each dough rectangle. Pinch dough to seal seams. Slice each rolled rectangle into 12 equal pieces. Place each piece, cut side up, in prepared muffin cups.
4. Bake for 10 minutes or until golden. Cool in muffin cups for 1 minute. Carefully remove rolls from muffin cups and arrange on a serving platter; cool slightly. Drizzle warm rolls with Honey Icing. Sprinkle with the reserved almonds.

Honey Icing In a small bowl stir together 1 cup powdered sugar, 2 tablespoons honey, and 1 tablespoon milk. If necessary, stir in additional milk, 1 teaspoon at a time, to reach drizzling consistency.

PER SERVING *75 cal., 3 g fat (1 g sat. fat), 3 mg chol., 84 mg sodium, 12 g carb., 0 g fiber, 1 g pro.*

Cinnamon-Chocolate Rolls with Hazelnuts

PREP 40 minutes
RISE 1 hour 15 minutes
BAKE 25 minutes at 375°F
COOL 10 minutes MAKES 12 servings

3¾ to 4¼ cups unbleached all-purpose flour
1 package active dry yeast
1 cup whole milk
⅔ cup sugar
¼ cup butter
1 teaspoon salt
1 egg
1 cup purchased chocolate-hazelnut spread
¼ cup butter, melted
1 tablespoon ground cinnamon
⅓ to ½ cup whipping cream
¼ cup hazelnuts (filberts), toasted and chopped (tip, page 64)

1. In a large mixing bowl stir together 1¼ cups of the flour and the yeast. In a medium saucepan heat and stir milk, ⅓ cup of the sugar, the ¼ cup butter, and salt just until warm (120°F to 130°F) and butter is almost melted. Add milk mixture to flour mixture; add egg. Beat with a mixer on low

to medium for 30 seconds, scraping sides of bowl constantly. Beat on high for 3 minutes. Stir in as much of the remaining flour as you can.
2. Turn dough out onto a lightly floured surface. Knead in enough of the remaining flour to make a moderately soft dough that is smooth and elastic (3 to 5 minutes total). Shape dough into a ball. Place in a lightly greased bowl, turning once to grease surface of dough. Cover and let rise in a warm place until double in size (45 to 60 minutes).
3. Punch dough down. Turn out onto a lightly floured surface. Cover and let rest for 10 minutes. Meanwhile, lightly grease a 13×9×2-inch baking pan; set aside. For fillings, in a small bowl combine ½ cup of the chocolate-hazelnut spread and ¼ cup melted butter. In another small bowl combine the remaining sugar and the cinnamon.
4. Roll dough into a 15×10-inch rectangle. Spread chocolate-hazelnut filling evenly over dough, leaving about ½ inch unfilled along the long sides. Sprinkle with cinnamon-sugar. Roll up rectangle, starting from a filled long side; pinch dough to seal seam. Cut into 12 slices. Arrange slices in baking pan. Cover and let rise in a warm place until nearly double in size (about 30 minutes).
5. Preheat oven to 375°F. Bake for 25 minutes or until golden. Cool in pan on wire rack for 10 minutes; remove from pan.
6. For icing, in a small bowl combine the remaining ½ cup chocolate-hazelnut spread and ⅓ cup of the whipping cream. If necessary, stir in additional whipping cream to reach drizzling consistency. Drizzle rolls with icing and sprinkle with hazelnuts. Serve warm.

PER SERVING *447 cal., 20 g fat (9 g sat. fat), 47 mg chol., 290 mg sodium, 58 g carb., 2 g fiber, 8 g pro.*

NUTTY HONEY MINI ROLLS

CINNAMON-
CHOCOLATE ROLLS
WITH HAZELNUTS

ORANGE-SPICED
COFFEE

Chocolate-Pecan Coffee Cake

PREP 30 minutes
BAKE 55 minutes at 325°F
COOL 20 minutes
MAKES 12 servings

½ cup butter, softened
1 cup granulated sugar
2 teaspoons baking powder
½ teaspoon baking soda
¼ teaspoon salt
2 eggs
1 teaspoon vanilla
2¼ cups all-purpose flour
1 8-ounce carton sour cream
1 recipe Coconut-Pecan Topping

1. Preheat oven to 325°F. Grease and flour a 10-inch fluted tube pan; set aside. In a large mixing bowl beat butter with a mixer on medium to high for 30 seconds. Add sugar, baking powder, baking soda, and salt. Beat until well combined, scraping sides of bowl occasionally. Add eggs one at a time, beating well after each addition. Beat in vanilla. Alternately add flour and sour cream to butter mixture, beating on low after each addition just until combined.
2. Sprinkle half the Coconut-Pecan Topping in the tube pan. Spoon half the cake batter in mounds over the topping. Carefully spread to an even layer. Sprinkle with remaining Coconut-Pecan Topping. Spoon on remaining cake batter and spread evenly.
3. Bake for 55 to 65 minutes or until a long wooden skewer inserted near the center comes out clean. Cool on a wire rack for 20 minutes. Invert cake and remove pan. Serve warm.
Coconut-Pecan Topping In a large bowl combine 1 cup flour, 1 cup packed brown sugar, and 1 teaspoon ground cinnamon. Cut in ½ cup cold butter until mixture resembles coarse crumbs; stir in ¾ cup semisweet chocolate pieces, ½ cup flaked coconut, and ½ cup chopped pecans.
PER SERVING *550 cal., 28 g fat (16 g sat. fat), 86 mg chol., 297 mg sodium, 71 g carb., 2 g fiber, 6 g pro.*

Orange-Spiced Coffee

START TO FINISH 25 minutes
MAKES 8 servings

⅓ cup ground coffee
2 orange slices
½ teaspoon ground cinnamon
¼ teaspoon ground nutmeg
⅛ teaspoon ground cloves
Cold water
½ cup half-and-half or light cream
2 tablespoons packed brown sugar
2 tablespoons orange liqueur (optional)
Orange slices (optional)
Cinnamon sticks (optional)

1. Place a coffee filter in the filter basket of a 10-cup electric drip coffeemaker. Place ground coffee, 2 orange slices, cinnamon, nutmeg, and cloves in the coffee filter. Fill coffee brewer (according to manufacturer's directions) with cold water to brew 10 cups.
2. Place pot on heating element; let water drip through basket. When dripping stops, remove pot from heat. Stir half-and-half, brown sugar, and, if desired, liqueur into brewed coffee.
3. Serve coffee in cups. If desired, garnish with additional orange slices and cinnamon sticks.
PER SERVING *44 cal., 2 g fat (1 g sat. fat), 6 mg chol., 9 mg sodium, 6 g carb., 0 g fiber, 1 g pro.*

Strawberry Smash

PREP 15 minutes
CHILL 1 hour 15 minutes
MAKES 8 servings

1 cup fresh strawberries, sliced
1 cup strawberry-flavor soda
2 tablespoons lime juice
1 tablespoon sugar
½ to ¾ cup whiskey, such as Jack Daniel's
1 750-milliliter bottle sparkling dry white wine, such as Prosecco, chilled
2 cups sparkling water, chilled
Sliced fresh strawberries (optional)

1. In a medium bowl combine the 1 cup sliced strawberries, soda, lime juice, and sugar. Cover and chill for 1 to 24 hours, stirring occasionally. Slightly crush berries with a muddler or fork; strain and discard seeds.
2. Transfer Strawberry Smash to a pitcher. Stir in whiskey. Cover and chill for 15 minutes.
3. Before serving, slowly pour sparkling wine and sparkling water into pitcher with Strawberry Smash; stir gently. Serve in champagne flutes. If desired, garnish with additional sliced strawberries.
PER SERVING *135 cal., 0 g fat, 0 mg chol., 21 mg sodium, 9 g carb., 0 g fiber, 0 g pro.*

STRAWBERRY SMASH

Yeast, Quick, and Little Breads

HOMEMADE BREAD is so satisfying to make. The smell of it baking fills your home with warmth and welcome. This variety of breads suits any occasion or time slot you may have for baking—from sweet and speedy muffins to hearty whole-grain yeast breads that help you slow down and savor the season.

CITRUS-TOPPED
DOUBLE-BLUEBERRY
MUFFINS, PAGE 73

CHEESY
SAUSAGE
BREAD

Cheesy Sausage Bread

PREP 30 minutes RISE 1 hour
STAND 10 minutes
BAKE 35 minutes at 350°F
COOL 5 minutes MAKES 16 servings

- 8 ounces bulk Italian sausage
- ¼ cup finely chopped onion
- 3¼ to 3¾ cups all-purpose flour
- 1 package active dry yeast
- 2 teaspoons dried Italian seasoning, crushed
- 1 cup milk
- ⅓ cup butter
- ¼ cup sugar
- ¾ teaspoon salt
- 1 egg
- 1½ cups shredded fontina cheese (6 ounces)
- 1½ cups shredded mozzarella cheese (6 ounces)
- ½ cup finely shredded Parmesan cheese (2 ounces)
- 1 cup basil pesto

1. In a large skillet cook sausage and onion over medium-high heat until meat is brown, using a wooden spoon to break up meat as it cooks. Drain off fat. Cover and chill sausage mixture until needed.
2. In a large mixing bowl stir together 1¼ cups of the flour, the yeast, and Italian seasoning. In a medium saucepan heat and stir milk, butter, sugar, and salt just until warm (120°F to 130°F) and butter almost melts. Add milk mixture to flour mixture; add egg. Beat with a mixer on low to medium for 30 seconds, scraping sides of bowl constantly. Beat on high for 3 minutes. Using a wooden spoon, stir in as much of the remaining flour as you can.
3. Turn dough out onto a lightly floured surface. Knead in enough of the remaining flour to make a moderately stiff dough that is smooth and elastic (6 to 8 minutes total). Shape dough into a ball. Place in a lightly greased bowl, turning once to grease surface of dough. Cover and let rise in a warm place until double in size (about 1 hour).
4. Punch dough down. Turn out onto a lightly floured surface. Divide dough in thirds. Cover and let rest for 10 minutes. Meanwhile, preheat oven to 350°F. Line two 9×5×3-inch loaf pans with parchment paper; set aside.

5. In a medium bowl combine sausage mixture, fontina cheese, mozzarella cheese, and Parmesan cheese; set aside.
6. Roll each portion of dough into a 30-inch-long rope. Cut ropes into 1-inch pieces. Divide one-third of the pieces between the prepared loaf pans. Divide one-third of the cheese mixture between pans. Repeat layers twice.
7. Bake for 35 to 40 minutes or until golden. Cool in pans on wire racks for 5 minutes. Remove loaves from pans; peel off parchment paper. Serve warm with pesto.
PER SERVING *365 cal., 23 g fat (10 g sat. fat), 62 mg chol., 606 mg sodium, 26 g carb., 1 g fiber, 14 g pro.*

Almond and Fennel Wheat Bread

PREP 35 minutes RISE 1½ hours
BAKE 30 minutes at 375°F
STAND 10 minutes
MAKES 12 servings

- 1⅓ cups warm water (105°F to 115°F)
- 1 package active dry yeast
- 1 teaspoon sugar
- 1 tablespoon olive oil
- 2 teaspoons fennel seeds, crushed
- 1½ teaspoons salt
- 1 cup whole wheat flour
- ½ cup chopped almonds or hazelnuts (filberts), toasted (tip, page 64)
- 2¼ to 2¾ cups bread flour or all-purpose flour

1. In a large bowl stir together the warm water, yeast, and sugar; let stand for 5 minutes. Add olive oil, fennel seeds, and salt.
2. Stir in the whole wheat flour. Stir in nuts and as much of the bread flour as you can. Turn dough out onto a lightly floured surface. Knead in enough remaining bread flour to make a moderately stiff dough that is smooth and elastic (6 to 8 minutes total). Shape the dough into a ball. Place dough in a lightly greased large bowl, turning once to grease surface.
3. Cover and let rise in a warm place until double in size (about 1 hour).
4. Punch dough down. Turn dough out onto a lightly floured surface. Cover and let rest for 10 minutes. Meanwhile, lightly grease a baking sheet. Shape dough into an 8×4-inch oval loaf. Place on prepared baking sheet. Sprinkle lightly with additional bread flour. Cover and let rise in a warm place until nearly double in size (30 to 45 minutes).
5. Preheat oven to 375°F. Using a sharp knife, slash top of loaf several times, making each cut about ½ inch deep. For a crisp crust, spray or brush the loaf with cold water. Bake about 30 minutes or until bread sounds hollow when lightly tapped, brushing or spraying with cold water halfway through baking. Immediately remove bread from pan. Cool on a wire rack.
PER SERVING *167 cal., 4 g fat (0 g sat. fat), 0 mg chol., 293 mg sodium, 28 g carb., 3 g fiber, 6 g pro.*

ALMOND AND FENNEL WHEAT BREAD

WHOLE GRAIN CARAMELIZED
ONION AND KALE BREAD

Whole Grain Caramelized Onion and Kale Bread

PREP 40 minutes RISE 1 hour
CHILL 2 hours STAND 30 minutes
BAKE 25 minutes at 350°F
MAKES 16 servings

  3 ounces pancetta, chopped
  1 tablespoon butter
  1 cup chopped onion
  ½ cup chopped ripe pear
  6 cloves garlic, minced
  2 cups chopped fresh kale
3½ to 4 cups all-purpose flour
  1 package active dry yeast
  1 teaspoon sea salt
1½ cups warm water (105°F to 115°F)
  4 ounces Gruyère cheese, shredded
  ½ cup whole wheat flour
  ½ cup ground rolled oats*
  ½ cup flaxseed
  1 egg
  1 teaspoon honey
  1 teaspoon water

1. In a large nonstick skillet cook pancetta over medium heat until crisp. Using a slotted spoon, transfer pancetta to a small bowl, reserving drippings in skillet. Add butter to drippings in skillet. Add onion, pear, and garlic; cook for 5 minutes or until tender. Stir in kale and pancetta; cook until kale is tender. Remove from heat; cool.
2. In a large mixing bowl combine 1 cup of the all-purpose flour, the yeast, and salt. Add the 1½ cups warm water. Beat with a mixer on low to medium for 30 seconds, scraping sides of bowl constantly. Beat on high for 3 minutes. Stir in cooled kale mixture and cheese. Stir in whole wheat flour, ground oats, and flaxseed. Gradually stir in as much of the remaining all-purpose flour as you can.
3. Turn dough out onto a lightly floured surface. Knead in enough remaining all-purpose flour to make a moderately stiff dough that is smooth and elastic (6 to 8 minutes total). Shape dough into a ball. Place in a lightly greased bowl, turning once to grease surface. Cover; let rise in a warm place until double in size (about 1 hour).

4. Punch dough down. Turn dough out onto a lightly floured surface. Cover; let rest for 10 minutes. Line a baking sheet with parchment paper; set aside. Shape dough by gently pulling it into a ball, tucking edges under. Place dough round on prepared baking sheet. Flatten round slightly to about 9 inches in diameter. Cover. (To serve today, let rise in a warm place until nearly double in size [30 to 40 minutes]. Omit Step 5 and continue as directed in Step 6.)
5. Chill for at least 2 hours or up to 24 hours. Let stand at room temperature for 30 minutes before baking.
6. Preheat oven to 350°F. In a small bowl whisk together egg, honey, and the 1 teaspoon water; brush top of dough round with egg mixture. Bake for 25 to 30 minutes or until golden and bread sounds hollow when lightly tapped. Cool on a wire rack. Store in the refrigerator.
PER SERVING 229 cal., 7 g fat (3 g sat. fat), 27 mg chol., 237 mg sodium, 32 g carb., 3 g fiber, 9 g pro.
*Tip Place ⅔ cup rolled oats in a food processor or blender. Cover and process or blend until ground.

No-Knead Bread

PREP 25 minutes STAND 1 hour
CHILL 8 hours
BAKE 40 minutes at 425°F
MAKES 12 servings

1½ cups warm water (105°F to 115°F)
  1 teaspoon active dry yeast
2¾ cups bread flour
  2 tablespoons sugar
  2 tablespoons olive oil
1½ teaspoons salt

1. In a 2-quart ovengoing nonstick saucepan stir together the warm water and yeast until yeast is dissolved. Stir in flour, sugar, oil, and salt until combined. Cover with lid; let stand in a warm place for 1 hour. Stir down. Cover and chill overnight.

2. Before baking, let dough stand, uncovered, at room temperature for 30 minutes. Preheat oven to 425°F. Bake in the saucepan, uncovered, about 40 minutes or until top is golden, bread sounds hollow when lightly tapped, and a thermometer inserted in the center registers 200°F. If necessary to prevent overbrowning, cover loosely with foil during the last 15 minutes of baking.
3. Immediately loosen sides and remove bread from saucepan. Cool on a wire rack.
PER SERVING 142 cal., 3 g fat (0 g sat. fat), 0 mg chol., 292 mg sodium, 25 g carb., 1 g fiber, 4 g pro.
Cheesy Bacon Bread Prepare as directed, except stir in ½ cup shredded Gouda cheese (2 ounces), ¼ cup crisp-cooked and crumbled bacon, 2 tablespoons coarse ground mustard, and 1 teaspoon caraway seeds, toasted, with the flour. Store, covered, in the refrigerator.
Cinnamon-Raisin Bread Prepare as directed, except stir in ½ cup raisins and ½ teaspoon ground cinnamon with the flour. Cover loosely with foil during the last 15 minutes of baking.
*Tip For traditional loaf-shape bread, use an 8×4×2-inch loaf pan instead of the saucepan. Line the loaf pan with parchment paper. Mix the dough in a large bowl and transfer to the prepared loaf pan; cover with greased or nonstick foil during standing and chilling in Step 1. Bake about 35 minutes or until top is golden, bread sounds hollow when lightly tapped, and a thermometer inserted in the center registers 200°F.

Easy Focaccia Casserole Bread

PREP **20 minutes** RISE **25 minutes**
BAKE **30 minutes at 375°F**
MAKES **12 servings**

- 3 cups all-purpose flour
- 1 package fast-rising active dry yeast
- 1 cup lukewarm water (120°F to 130°F)
- 1 egg
- 1 tablespoon sugar
- 1 tablespoon olive oil
- ½ teaspoon salt
  Olive oil
- ½ teaspoon Italian seasoning, crushed
  Grated Romano cheese (optional)
- 2 tablespoons sliced green onion (optional)
- 2 tablespoons kalamata olives, quartered lengthwise (optional)

1. Grease a 1½-quart casserole well; set aside. In a medium mixing bowl combine 1½ cups of the flour and the yeast. Add the water, egg, sugar, the 1 tablespoon olive oil, and the salt. Beat with a mixer on low for 30 seconds, scraping sides of bowl constantly. Beat on high for 3 minutes. Using a wooden spoon, stir in the remaining 1½ cups flour (batter will be stiff).

2. Spoon batter into casserole. Brush top with additional olive oil. Sprinkle with Italian seasoning. If desired, sprinkle with cheese, green onion, and olives. Cover; let rise in a warm place until nearly double in size (25 to 30 minutes).

3. Preheat oven to 375°F. Bake for 30 to 35 minutes or until bread sounds hollow when lightly tapped. Remove from casserole; cool completely on a wire rack.

PER SERVING *145 cal., 3 g fat (0 g sat. fat), 18 mg chol., 104 mg sodium, 25 g carb., 1 g fiber, 4 g pro.*

Dark Chocolate-Hazelnut Casserole Bread

PREP **25 minutes** RISE **2 hours**
BAKE **50 minutes at 350°F**
COOL **10 minutes**
MAKES **18 servings**

- 3½ cups all-purpose flour
- ⅓ cup packed brown sugar
- 1 package active dry yeast
- ¾ teaspoon salt
- ¼ teaspoon instant espresso coffee powder
- ¾ cup evaporated milk
- 5 tablespoons butter
- ¼ cup water
- 2 eggs
- 6 ounces dark or bittersweet chocolate, chopped (1 cup)
- ½ cup toasted hazelnuts (filberts)*, coarsely chopped
- 1 tablespoon water
- 1 tablespoon turbinado sugar (optional)

1. In a large mixing bowl combine 2 cups of the flour, the brown sugar, yeast, salt, and coffee powder; set aside.

2. In a small saucepan heat and stir evaporated milk, butter, and ¼ cup water just until warm (120°F to 130°F) and butter is almost melted. Add milk mixture to flour mixture; add one of the eggs. Beat with a mixer on low for 30 seconds, scraping sides of bowl constantly. Beat on high for 3 minutes. Stir in chocolate and hazelnuts. Using a wooden spoon, stir in as much of the remaining flour as needed to make a soft, sticky dough. Cover and let rise in a warm place until double in size (about 1 hour).

3. Grease a 2-quart oval or square baking dish. Punch dough down. Transfer dough to the prepared baking dish. Cover and let rise in a warm place until double in size (about 1 hour).

4. Preheat oven to 350°F. In a small bowl combine the remaining egg and the 1 tablespoon water. Brush top of loaf with egg mixture. If desired, sprinkle with turbinado sugar.

5. Bake for 50 to 55 minutes or until loaf sounds hollow when lightly tapped. (If necessary, cover loosely with foil during the last 15 minutes of baking to prevent overbrowning.) Cool in dish on a wire rack for 10 minutes. Remove bread from dish; cool completely on rack.

PER SERVING *227 cal., 11 g fat (5 g sat. fat), 35 mg chol., 141 mg sodium, 29 g carb., 2 g fiber, 5 g pro.*

*Tip To toast hazelnuts, preheat oven to 350°F. Spread nuts in a single layer in a shallow baking pan. Bake for 8 to 10 minutes or until lightly toasted, stirring once to toast evenly. Cool nuts slightly then place on a clean kitchen towel; rub with the towel to remove the loose skins.

EASY FOCACCIA CASSEROLE BREAD

DARK CHOCOLATE-
HAZELNUT CASSEROLE
BREAD

Best Cinnamon Rolls

PREP **45 minutes** RISE **2 hours**
BAKE **25 minutes at 350°F**
MAKES **24 servings**

  2 packages active dry yeast
2½ cups lukewarm water (105°F
       to 115°F)
  1 teaspoon sugar
  1 package white cake mix
  6 cups all-purpose flour
  1 egg
  ⅓ cup vegetable oil
  ½ teaspoon salt
  ¼ cup butter, melted
  1 cup sugar
  4 teaspoons ground cinnamon
  1 recipe Powdered Sugar Icing

1. For dough, in a very large mixing bowl, stir the yeast into ½ cup of the warm water; add the 1 teaspoon sugar. Let stand for 5 minutes or until foamy.
2. Stir the cake mix, 1 cup of the flour, the egg, oil, salt, and remaining water into yeast mixture. Beat with a mixer on high for 3 minutes, scraping sides of bowl constantly. Stir in the remaining flour to form a soft dough. (Dough will be sticky.)
3. Cover and let rise about 1 hour or until doubled.
4. Lightly grease two 13×9×2-inch baking pans. Set aside. Stir dough down. Cover and let rise again until doubled (about 30 minutes). Stir dough again. Divide in half. Turn one portion of the dough onto a well-

floured surface*. Turn to coat lightly with flour. Roll or pat the dough into a 12×8-inch rectangle. Brush with half the melted butter.
5. For filling, in a small mixing bowl combine the 1 cup sugar and the cinnamon. Sprinkle half the filling over dough. Roll up, jelly-roll style, starting from one long side. Pinch edge to seal. Cut crosswise into 12 pieces. Arrange, cut sides down, in a prepared pan. Repeat with the remaining dough, butter, and filling. Cover loosely; let the dough rise in a warm place until nearly doubled (about 30 to 45 minutes).
6. Preheat oven to 350°F. Uncover pans. Place a baking sheet under each pan. Bake for 25 to 30 minutes or until lightly browned and rolls sound hollow when lightly tapped. Invert onto serving plates. Drizzle Powdered Sugar Icing over warm rolls. Serve warm.
Powdered Sugar Icing In a medium bowl stir together 4 cups powdered sugar, 1 teaspoon vanilla, and enough milk (3 to 4 tablespoons) to make drizzling consistency.

PER SERVING *356 cal., 8 g fat (2 g sat. fat), 14 mg chol., 213 mg sodium, 67 g carb., 1 g fiber, 5 g pro.*

***Tip** For easier handling, chill dough 1 hour before rolling or patting out.
German Chocolate Pecan Rolls Prepare dough as for Best Cinnamon Rolls, except substitute 1 package (2-layer size) dark chocolate cake mix for the white cake mix. For filling, omit cinnamon and add 1¼ cups miniature semisweet chocolate pieces and 1 cup flaked or shredded coconut to the sugar. Shape rolls as directed. In a saucepan melt ⅔ cup butter. Stir in 1⅓ cups packed brown sugar and ⅓ cup light-color corn syrup. Heat and stir until sugar is melted. Remove from heat. Stir in 2 cups coarsely chopped pecans. Divide pecan mixture between pans. Slice each roll of dough into 12 pieces. Arrange 12 pieces, cut sides down, in each prepared pan. Let rise and bake as directed. Turn out rolls onto serving platter immediately after baking. Omit Powdered Sugar Icing.

Apple-Pumpkin Sunflower Bread

PREP 30 minutes
BAKE 55 minutes at 350°F
COOL 10 minutes MAKES 32 servings

1½ cups whole wheat flour or white whole wheat flour
1½ cups all-purpose flour
2¼ teaspoons pumpkin pie spice
2 teaspoons baking soda
1 teaspoon salt
1 cup granulated sugar
1 cup packed brown sugar
1 cup walnut oil or vegetable oil
4 eggs
½ cup boiled cider, applejack, apple brandy, apple cider, or apple juice
1 15-ounce can pumpkin
1½ cups finely chopped, peeled firm, sweet apples (such as Golden Delicious, Jonagold, Pink Lady, Braeburn, and/or Cameo)
½ cup dry-roasted sunflower seeds or chopped walnuts

1. Preheat oven to 350°F. Grease the bottom and ½ inch up the sides of two 9×5×3-inch, three 8×4×2-inch, or four 7½×3½×2-inch loaf pans. Line bottoms with parchment paper; grease parchment. In a large bowl combine flours, pumpkin pie spice, baking soda, and salt.

2. In an extra-large mixing bowl combine granulated sugar, brown sugar, and oil. Beat with a mixer on medium until well mixed. Add eggs; beat well. Alternately add flour mixture and boiled cider to sugar mixture, beating on low after each addition just until combined. Beat in pumpkin. Fold in apples and sunflower seeds. Spoon batter into prepared pans; spread evenly.

3. Bake 55 to 60 minutes for the 9×5-inch loaves, 45 to 50 minutes for 8×4-inch loaves or 40 to 45 minutes for 7½×3½-inch loaves, or until a toothpick inserted near centers comes out clean.

4. Cool in pans on wire racks for 10 minutes. Remove from pans; remove parchment. Cool completely on wire racks. Wrap and store overnight before slicing.

PER SERVING 180 cal., 9 g fat (1 g sat. fat), 23 mg chol., 173 mg sodium, 24 g carb., 1 g fiber, 3 g pro.

APPLE-PUMPKIN SUNFLOWER BREAD

TANGERINE-POPPY
SEED QUICK BREAD

Tangerine-Poppy Seed Quick Bread

PREP **20 minutes**
BAKE **50 minutes at 350°F**
COOL **10 minutes** STAND **10 minutes**
MAKES **16 servings**

- 2 cups all-purpose flour
- 1 cup sugar
- 2 teaspoons baking powder
- ½ teaspoon salt
- 1 egg, lightly beaten
- 1 cup milk
- ¼ cup vegetable oil
- 1 tablespoon finely shredded tangerine peel
- 2 tablespoons tangerine juice
- 1 tablespoon poppy seeds
- 2 tablespoons sugar
- 2 tablespoons tangerine juice
- 1 tablespoon butter

1. Preheat oven to 350°F. Grease the bottom and ½ inch up the sides of an 8×4×2-inch loaf pan. In a large bowl stir together flour, the 1 cup sugar, the baking powder, and salt. Make a well in the center of flour mixture; set aside.
2. In a medium bowl combine egg, milk, oil, tangerine zest, 2 tablespoons tangerine juice, and poppy seeds. Add egg mixture all at once to flour mixture. Stir just until moistened (batter should be lumpy). Spoon batter into the prepared loaf pan.
3. Bake for 50 to 55 minutes or until a wooden toothpick inserted near center comes out clean. Cool in pan on a wire rack for 10 minutes.
4. Meanwhile, for tangerine glaze, in a small saucepan combine the 2 tablespoons sugar, 2 tablespoons tangerine juice, and butter. Stir over medium-low heat until butter is melted and sugar is dissolved.
5. Remove bread from pan. Poke holes in top of warm bread with a wooden skewer; slowly brush with tangerine glaze. Cool completely on a wire rack. Wrap and store overnight before slicing.
PER SERVING *164 cal., 5 g fat (1 g sat. fat), 15 mg chol., 121 mg sodium, 27 g carb., 1 g fiber, 3 g pro.*

APPLE PIE BREAD

Apple Pie Bread

PREP **35 minutes**
BAKE **1 hour at 350°F**
COOL **10 minutes**
MAKES **14 servings**

- ½ cup butter, softened
- 1 cup sugar
- ¼ cup buttermilk or sour milk*
- 2 teaspoons baking powder
- 2 eggs
- 1 teaspoon vanilla
- 2 cups all-purpose flour
- ½ teaspoon salt
- 2 cups shredded, peeled apples (about 4 medium)
- 1 cup chopped walnuts or pecans
- ½ cup raisins
- 1 recipe Streusel-Nut Topping

1. Preheat oven to 350°F. Grease the bottom and ½ inch up the sides of a 9×5×3-inch loaf pan; set aside.
2. In a large mixing bowl beat butter with a mixer on medium to high for 30 seconds. Beat in sugar until combined. Add buttermilk and baking powder; beat until combined. Add eggs and vanilla; beat until combined. Add flour and salt; beat until combined. Stir in apples, nuts, and raisins. Spoon batter into prepared pan. Sprinkle Streusel-Nut Topping over batter.
3. Bake for 60 to 65 minutes or until a wooden toothpick inserted near center comes out clean. Cool in pan on a wire rack for 10 minutes. Remove bread from pan. Cool completely on wire rack. Wrap and store overnight before slicing.
Streusel-Nut Topping In a small bowl stir together ¼ cup packed brown sugar and 3 tablespoons all-purpose flour. Cut in 3 tablespoons butter until mixture resembles coarse crumbs. Stir in ⅓ cup chopped walnuts or pecans.
PER SERVING *326 cal., 17 g fat (6 g sat. fat), 52 mg chol., 193 mg sodium, 42 g carb., 2 g fiber, 5 g pro.*
*****Tip** To make ¼ cup sour milk, place ¾ teaspoon lemon juice or vinegar in a glass measuring cup. Add enough milk to equal ¼ cup total liquid; stir. Let stand for 5 minutes before using.
To Store Wrap cooled loaf in foil or plastic wrap. Refrigerate up to 1 week. Or place loaf in freezer bag or container and freeze up to 3 months. Thaw frozen loaf overnight in the refrigerator.

Cranberry-Pumpkin Scones with Sugared Pepitas

PREP 30 minutes
BAKE 15 minutes at 400°F
COOL 5 minutes
MAKES 28 servings

2½ cups all-purpose flour
¼ cup packed brown sugar
2 teaspoons baking powder
1½ teaspoons pumpkin pie spice
¼ teaspoon baking soda
¼ teaspoon salt
½ cup butter, cut up
½ cup dried cranberries
2 eggs, lightly beaten
½ cup half-and-half, light cream, or milk
½ cup canned pumpkin
1 egg, lightly beaten
1 tablespoon water
2 cups powdered sugar
1 tablespoon butter, softened
2 teaspoons orange zest
2 tablespoons orange juice
1 recipe Sugared Pepitas
Finely shredded orange peel (optional)

1. Preheat oven to 400°F. Line a large baking sheet with parchment paper; set aside. In a large bowl stir together flour, brown sugar, baking powder, pumpkin pie spice, baking soda, and salt. Using a pastry blender, cut in the ½ cup butter until mixture resembles coarse crumbs. Add cranberries and toss well. Make a well in the center of the flour mixture.

2. In a small bowl stir together the 2 eggs, half-and-half, and pumpkin. Add pumpkin mixture all at once to flour mixture. Using a fork, stir just until moistened.

3. Turn dough out onto a well-floured surface. Knead dough by folding and gently pressing for 10 to 12 strokes or until dough is nearly smooth. Pat or lightly roll dough into an 8-inch circle. Cut circle into eight wedges.

4. Place wedges 2 inches apart on the prepared baking sheet. In a small bowl combine the 1 egg with the 1 tablespoon water. Brush wedges lightly with egg mixture. Bake for 15 to 20 minutes or until golden. Remove scones from baking sheet. Cool for 5 minutes before spreading with glaze.

5. For glaze, in a small bowl stir together powdered sugar, the 1 tablespoon butter, the 2 teaspoons orange zest, and the orange juice until well combined.

6. Spoon glaze over warm scones. Sprinkle with some of the Sugared Pepitas and, if desired, additional shredded orange peel. Serve warm.

Sugared Pepitas Preheat oven to 325°F. Line a 15×10×1-inch baking pan with parchment paper; set aside. In a small saucepan combine ⅓ cup sugar and 2 tablespoons water. Cook and stir over medium-high heat until sugar is dissolved; remove from heat. Let cool. In a medium bowl combine 1 cup raw pepitas with cooled sugar mixture; toss well to combine. Spread in prepared baking pan. Sprinkle with 1 tablespoon sugar and ¼ teaspoon salt. Bake for 15 to 20 minutes or until lightly browned and crisp, stirring twice. Cool on baking sheet. Makes 2 cups.

PER SERVING 544 cal., 21 g fat (11 g sat. fat), 119 mg chol., 401 mg sodium, 82 g carb., 2 g fiber, 9 g pro.

CRANBERRY-PUMPKIN SCONES WITH SUGARED PEPITAS

CHOCOLATE-AND-
GINGER-SPIKED
SCONES

Chocolate-and Ginger-Spiked Scones

PREP 30 minutes
BAKE 15 minutes at 400°F
MAKES 10 servings

2 cups all-purpose flour
¼ cup sugar
1½ teaspoons baking powder
½ teaspoon ground ginger
⅛ teaspoon salt
¼ cup cold butter, cut up
¼ cup chopped bittersweet or semisweet chocolate
2 tablespoons chopped crystallized ginger
2 egg whites, lightly beaten
⅓ cup fat-free milk
Nonstick cooking spray
Fat-free milk
Coarse sugar (optional)

1. Preheat oven to 400°F. In a medium bowl stir together flour, sugar, baking powder, ground ginger, and salt. Using a pastry blender, cut in butter until mixture resembles coarse crumbs. Stir in chocolate and crystallized ginger. Make a well in the center of the flour mixture.
2. In a small bowl stir together egg whites and ⅓ cup fat-free milk. Add milk mixture all at once to flour mixture. Stir just until moistened. Turn dough out onto a lightly floured surface. Knead dough by folding and gently pressing 10 to 12 strokes, until nearly smooth.
3. Divide dough in half. Roll or pat each dough half into a 5-inch circle. Cut each circle into five wedges. Lightly coat baking sheet with nonstick cooking spray; place wedges on a baking sheet. Brush with additional milk. If desired, sprinkle with coarse sugar. Bake for 15 minutes or until bottoms are browned. Serve warm.

PER SERVING *187 cal., 6 g fat (4 g sat. fat), 13 mg chol., 133 mg sodium, 29 g carb., 1 g fiber, 4 g pro.*

STRAWBERRY CREAM
SCUFFINS

Strawberry Cream Scuffins

PREP **40 minutes**
BAKE **25 minutes at 350°F**
COOL **5 minutes**
MAKES **18 servings**

Nonstick cooking spray
1 egg, lightly beaten
1 cup whipping cream or milk
3 cups all-purpose flour
2 tablespoons sugar
1 tablespoon baking powder
¼ teaspoon salt
½ cup butter
1 cup finely chopped fresh strawberries
6 tablespoons strawberry jelly, jam, or preserves
1 recipe Scuffin Icing
Chopped fresh strawberries (optional)

1. Preheat oven to 350°F. Line eighteen 2½-inch muffin cups with paper bake cups; coat bake cups with cooking spray. In a small bowl combine egg and whipping cream.
2. In a large bowl stir together flour, sugar, baking powder, and salt. Using a pastry blender, cut in butter until mixture resembles coarse crumbs. Stir in the 1 cup strawberries. Make a well in the center of flour mixture. Reserve 2 tablespoons of the egg mixture. Add the remaining egg mixture all at once to flour mixture. Using a fork, stir just until moistened (dough will be crumbly).
3. Spoon half the dough into the prepared muffin cups, filling each one-third full. Using a spoon or your thumb, make an indentation in the center of dough in each cup; fill each indentation with 1 teaspoon of the strawberry jelly. Spoon the remaining dough into muffin cups. Brush with the reserved 2 tablespoons egg mixture.
4. Bake about 25 minutes or until tops are golden. Cool in muffin cups on wire racks for 5 minutes. Remove from muffin cups. Drizzle with Scuffin Icing. If desired, top with additional strawberries. Serve warm.
Scuffin Icing In a small bowl stir together ½ cup powdered sugar, 2 teaspoons whipping cream or milk, and ¼ teaspoon vanilla. Stir in enough additional whipping cream or milk, 1 teaspoon at a time, to reach drizzling consistency.
PER SERVING *215 cal., 11 g fat (7 g sat. fat), 43 mg chol., 171 mg sodium, 27 g carb., 1 g fiber, 3 g pro.*

Citrus-Topped Double-Blueberry Muffins

PREP **15 minutes**
BAKE **20 minutes at 375°F**
COOL **10 minutes**
makes **12 servings**

2 cups all-purpose flour
¾ cup sugar
2½ teaspoons baking powder
¼ teaspoon salt
2 eggs
¾ cup buttermilk or milk
6 tablespoons butter, melted
1 cup fresh or frozen blueberries
½ cup blueberry preserves
1 teaspoon orange zest
1 teaspoon lemon zest
2 tablespoons sugar
2 tablespoons butter, melted

1. Preheat oven to 375°F. Line twelve 2½-inch muffin cups with paper bake cups.
2. In a medium mixing bowl stir together flour, the ¾ cup sugar, baking powder, and salt. Make a well in center of flour mixture.
3. Whisk together eggs, buttermilk, and 6 tablespoons melted butter; add all at once to flour. Stir just until moistened (batter should be lumpy). Fold in blueberries. Remove 1 cup of batter.
4. Spoon remaining batter into prepared muffin cups, filling about half full. Spoon 2 teaspoons blueberry preserves into the center of each muffin. Top with remaining batter, filling cups about two-thirds full. Bake 20 minutes or until golden.
5. Meanwhile, stir together orange and lemon zest and 2 tablespoons sugar. Remove muffins from oven; brush with 2 tablespoons melted butter. Sprinkle citrus-sugar mixture on top. Cool on wire rack 10 minutes. Serve warm.
PER SERVING *263 cal., 9 g fat (5 g sat. fat), 52 mg chol., 225 mg sodium, 43 g carb., 1 g fiber, 4 g pro.*

CITRUS-TOPPED DOUBLE-BLUEBERRY MUFFINS

All Things Sweet

INDULGENT DESSERTS are one of the greatest pleasures of the holiday season. You'll find something for everyone in these recipes that span the spectrum of sweets, from eye-popping cakes to an array of pies and tarts to fabulous fruit desserts.

POLKA-DOT CAKE,
PAGE 78

BANANA PUDDING CAKE ROLL

Banana Pudding Cake Roll

PREP 30 minutes STAND 30 minutes
BAKE 12 minutes at 375°F
CHILL 2 hours MAKES 10 servings

 3 eggs
 ¾ cup all-purpose flour
 1 teaspoon baking powder
 1 teaspoon ground cinnamon
 ½ teaspoon salt
 1 cup granulated sugar
 ⅔ cup mashed bananas (2 medium)
   Powdered sugar
 ¼ cup granulated sugar
 1 tablespoon cornstarch
 1 cup milk
 1 egg yolk, lightly beaten
 1 teaspoon butter
 ½ teaspoon vanilla
 2 ripe bananas, sliced ¼ inch thick
 1 recipe Marshmallow Frosting

1. Allow eggs to stand at room temperature for 30 minutes. Meanwhile, grease a 15×10×1-inch baking pan. Line bottom of pan with waxed paper or parchment paper; grease paper.
2. Preheat oven to 375°F. In a small bowl stir together flour, baking powder, cinnamon, and salt. In a large mixing bowl beat eggs with a mixer on high for 5 minutes or until thick and lemon color. Gradually add 1 cup granulated sugar, beating on medium until light and fluffy. Stir in mashed bananas. Beat in flour mixture on low to medium just until combined. Spread batter evenly in the baking pan.
3. Bake for 12 to 15 minutes or until cake springs back when lightly touched. Immediately loosen edges of cake from pan and turn cake out onto a clean kitchen towel sprinkled with powdered sugar. Remove waxed paper. Roll towel and cake into a spiral, starting from a short side of the cake. Cool on a wire rack.
4. For filling, in a small heavy saucepan stir together ¼ cup granulated sugar and cornstarch. Gradually stir in milk. Cook and stir over medium heat until thickened and bubbly. Cook and stir for 2 minutes more. Remove from heat. Gradually stir about ⅓ cup of the hot mixture into egg yolk. Return egg yolk

mixture to saucepan. Bring to a gentle boil; reduce heat. Cook and stir for 2 minutes. Remove from heat. Stir in butter and vanilla. Pour filling into a bowl. Cover surface with plastic wrap; cool slightly.

5. Unroll cake; remove towel. Spread cake with filling to within 1 inch of the edges. Place banana slices in a single layer on filling. Roll up cake; trim ends. Cover and chill for at least 2 hours or until completely chilled.

6. Before serving, preheat broiler. Prepare Marshmallow Frosting. Spread frosting over top and sides of cake roll, using the spatula to add peaks. Broil 6 to 8 inches from the heat for 1 to 2 minutes or until peaks start to brown along the edges.

Marshmallow Frosting In the top of a 2-quart double boiler combine ¾ cup sugar, 3 tablespoons cold water, 1 egg white, and ⅛ teaspoon cream of tartar. Beat with an electric mixer on low for 30 seconds. Place the pan over boiling water (upper pan should not touch the water). Cook, beating constantly with the mixer on high, for 10 to 13 minutes or until an instant-read thermometer inserted in the frosting registers 160°F, stopping mixer and quickly scraping bottom and sides of pan every 5 minutes to prevent sticking. Remove from heat; add 1 teaspoon vanilla. Beat 1 minute more or until frosting is fluffy and soft peaks form (tips curl).

PER SERVING *287 cal., 3 g fat (1 g sat. fat), 77 mg chol., 209 mg sodium, 62 g carb., 2 g fiber, 5 g pro.*

Citrus Upside-Down Cake

PREP **30 minutes**
STAND **30 minutes**
BAKE **45 minutes at 350°F**
COOL **20 minutes**
MAKES **20 servings**

4 eggs
1⅓ cups packed brown sugar
½ cup butter, melted
¼ cup water
5 to 6 oranges, grapefruit, and/or clementines, peeled and thinly sliced
2 cups all-purpose flour
2 teaspoons baking powder
½ teaspoon ground cardamom
2 cups granulated sugar
1 cup milk
¼ cup butter, cut up

1. Allow eggs to stand at room temperature for 30 minutes. Meanwhile, preheat oven to 350°F. In a medium bowl stir together brown sugar, the melted butter, and the water until combined; spread evenly over bottom of pan. Place fruit slices evenly on brown sugar mixture, overlapping as necessary. Set pan aside.
2. In a medium bowl stir together flour, baking powder, and ground cardamom; set aside. In a large mixing bowl beat eggs with a mixer on high for 4 minutes or until slightly thickened. Gradually beat in granulated sugar; beat on medium for 4 to 5 minutes

or until light and fluffy. Add flour mixture; beat on low to medium just until combined (batter will be thick).
3. In a small saucepan heat and stir milk and the ¼ cup butter until butter is melted; beat into batter until combined. Carefully pour batter over citrus slices.
4. Bake for 45 minutes or until a wooden toothpick inserted near the center comes out clean (avoid checking cake too early, it could sink in the center). Cool in pan on a wire rack for at least 20 minutes. Using a thin metal spatula, loosen sides of cake from pan; invert onto serving platter. Spoon remaining brown sugar sauce in pan over cake. Cool.

PER SERVING *277 cal., 8 g fat (5 g sat. fat), 56 mg chol., 134 mg sodium, 49 g carb., 1 g fiber, 3 g pro.*

CITRUS UPSIDE-DOWN CAKE

Polka-Dot Cake

(photo on page 74)

PREP 1 hour
BAKE 1½ hours at 350°F
STAND 30 minutes
COOL 2 hours 10 minutes
MAKES 16 servings

- 1 2-layer-size package white cake mix
- 2 tablespoons cocoa powder
- 1 1-ounce bottle liquid red food coloring
- 6 egg whites
- 3 cups all-purpose flour
- 1½ teaspoons baking powder
- 1 teaspoon salt
- ½ teaspoon baking soda
- ¾ cup shortening
- 2⅔ cups sugar
- 1½ teaspoons vanilla
- 2 cups buttermilk
- 1 recipe Almost-Homemade Vanilla Buttercream Frosting

1. Preheat oven to 350°F. Grease and flour the top and bottom cups of a 12-cup cake-pop pan. Prepare cake mix batter, adding the cocoa powder according to package directions. Beat in food coloring. Spoon 1 tablespoon of the batter into each bottom cup (without hole), filling each full. Place top half of pan on top and secure. Bake about 10 minutes or until a toothpick inserted into holes comes out clean. Cool in pan on a wire rack for 5 minutes. Remove top pan. Remove cake balls from pans; cool completely on wire rack. Wash, grease, and flour pan; repeat baking twice to make 36 cake balls total. (Cover and chill remaining batter to use for cupcakes, following package directions. Makes 12 cupcakes.)
2. Meanwhile, place egg whites in a small bowl; cover and let stand at room temperature for 30 minutes. Grease and flour a 10-inch tube pan with a removable bottom; set aside. In a medium bowl stir together flour, baking powder, salt, and baking soda; set aside. In a very large mixing bowl beat shortening with a mixer on medium to high for 30 seconds. Add sugar and vanilla. Beat for 3 minutes or until light. Add egg whites, one at a time, beating well after each addition. Alternately add flour mixture and buttermilk to beaten mixture, beating on low after each addition just until combined.
3. Arrange half of the cake balls in the prepared tube pan; to give the baked cake a polka-dot effect, stagger the balls in the pan. Spoon about 4 cups of the white batter over the balls. Add the remaining cake balls, staggering them. Spoon the remaining white batter into pan over cake balls. Place tube pan on a baking sheet. Bake for 60 to 70 minutes or until a long wooden skewer inserted into cake comes out clean. Remove and cool on a wire rack for 10 minutes. Using a sharp knife, loosen cake from sides of pan and tube. Remove sides of pan. Run the knife along the bottom of the cake to loosen from bottom of pan. Invert cake; remove tube and pan bottom. Cool on a wire rack about 2 hours or until completely cooled.
4. Prepare frosting. Place cake on a serving platter. Spread frosting on cooled cake and cupcakes.
Almost-Homemade Vanilla Buttercream Frosting In a large mixing bowl beat 1½ cups softened unsalted butter with a mixer on medium until light and fluffy. Add one 16-ounce jar marshmallow creme (or one 13-ounce jar plus ¾ cup additional marshmallow creme); beat until smooth, scraping sides of bowl occasionally. Add ½ cup powdered sugar and 1 teaspoon vanilla; beat until light and fluffy. (If frosting is too stiff to spread, soften in microwave no longer than 10 seconds, then beat again until light and fluffy.) If desired, store, covered, in the refrigerator up to 3 days. Bring to room temperature before using.
PER SERVING 538 cal., 17 g fat (6 g sat. fat), 24 mg chol., 452 mg sodium, 90 g carb., 2 g fiber, 7 g pro.

Dark Chocolate and Pumpkin Swirl Cake

PREP 30 minutes
BAKE 55 minutes at 350°F
STAND 20 minutes
MAKES 12 servings

Nonstick cooking spray
- 1¾ cups all-purpose flour
- 2 teaspoons pumpkin pie spice
- 1 teaspoon baking powder
- ½ teaspoon baking soda
- ½ teaspoon salt
- 2 large eggs
- 1¼ cups granulated sugar
- ½ cup unsalted butter, melted
- ½ cup buttermilk
- 2 teaspoons vanilla
- 1 cup canned pumpkin
- 3 ounces dark chocolate, melted
- 2 tablespoons unsweetened cocoa powder
- 1½ cups powdered sugar
- 1 teaspoon orange zest
- 2 to 3 tablespoons milk

1. Preheat oven to 350°F. Coat a 9×5-inch loaf pan with cooking spray. Line bottom of pan with parchment paper then coat with cooking spray.
2. In a large bowl whisk together flour, pumpkin pie spice, baking powder, baking soda, and salt.
3. In a medium bowl whisk together eggs and sugar. Whisk in melted butter, buttermilk, and vanilla. Fold in pumpkin.
4. Add the pumpkin mixture all at once to the flour mixture; whisk just until no lumps remain.
5. Divide batter in half. Add the melted chocolate and cocoa powder to half of the batter; stir to combine.
6. Add the two batters to the loaf pan, alternating between pumpkin and chocolate. Using a table knife, swirl through the batter. Bake for 55 to 65 minutes or until a toothpick inserted near the center comes out clean. Cool in pan for 20 minutes. Remove and cool completely on a wire rack.
7. In a small bowl stir together the powdered sugar, half the orange zest, and enough milk for drizzling consistency. Spoon over cooled loaf. Sprinkle remaining orange zest.
PER SERVING 341 cal., 12 g fat (7 g sat. fat), 53 mg chol., 216 mg sodium, 57 g carb., 2 g fiber, 4 g pro.

DARK CHOCOLATE
AND PUMPKIN
SWIRL CAKE

CRANBERRY-VANILLA BEAN
CAKE WITH LEMON CREAM
CHEESE FROSTING

Cranberry-Vanilla Bean Cake with Lemon Cream Cheese Frosting

PREP 35 minutes STAND 30 minutes
BAKE 25 minutes at 350°F
COOL 1 hour MAKES 14 servings

- 6 egg whites, lightly beaten
- 1 cup buttermilk
- 2¼ cups cake flour
- 1¾ cups sugar
- 4 teaspoons baking powder
- 1 teaspoon salt
- 1 vanilla bean, split lengthwise
- ¾ cup butter, softened
- 1 12-ounce package fresh or frozen cranberries, thawed
- ½ cup sugar
- 2 teaspoons orange zest
- 2 tablespoons orange juice
- ¼ teaspoon ground cinnamon
- ⅛ teaspoon ground ginger
- ⅛ teaspoon ground cloves
- 1 recipe Lemon Cream Cheese Frosting
- 1 recipe White Chocolate Curls (optional)

1. In a small bowl combine egg whites and buttermilk. Let stand at room temperature for 30 minutes. Meanwhile, grease and lightly flour two 9×1½-inch round cake pans. In a bowl stir together cake flour, 1¾ cups sugar, baking powder, and salt.
2. Preheat oven to 350°F. Using the tip of a small sharp knife, scrape seeds from vanilla bean. Stir seeds into buttermilk mixture.
3. In a large mixing bowl beat butter with a mixer on medium to high for 30 seconds. Using a wooden spoon, gradually stir in flour mixture until mixture resembles coarse crumbs. Stir in half of the buttermilk mixture until moistened. Add the remaining buttermilk mixture. Beat on medium for 2 minutes, scraping sides of bowl occasionally.
4. Pour batter into the prepared cake pans, spreading evenly. Bake for 25 to 30 minutes or until a wooden toothpick inserted near centers comes out clean. Cool in pans on wire racks for 10 minutes. Remove layers from pans; cool completely on wire racks.

5. For cranberry filling, in a medium saucepan combine cranberries, ½ cup sugar, orange zest, orange juice, cinnamon, ginger, and cloves. Bring to boiling; reduce heat. Simmer, uncovered, about 10 minutes or until cranberries pop and filling starts to thicken. Mash cranberries slightly with the back of a spoon or a potato masher. Transfer filling to a bowl; cool.
6. To assemble cake, cut each layer in half horizontally. Place one layer, cut side up, on a serving plate; spread with one-third of the cranberry filling. Top with a second cake layer; spread with ¾ cup of the Lemon Cream Cheese Frosting. Spread one-third of the cranberry filling on frosting. Top with a third cake layer; spread with the remaining cranberry filling. Top with the fourth cake layer, cut side down.
7. Frost top and sides of cake with the remaining frosting. If desired, garnish with White Chocolate Curls.

Lemon Cream Cheese Frosting In a large mixing bowl beat two 8-ounce packages softened cream cheese and ¾ cup softened butter with a mixer on medium until light and fluffy. Gradually beat in 1 cup powdered sugar. Beat in 1 tablespoon lemon zest and 1 tablespoon lemon juice. Gradually beat in 2½ cups powdered sugar. If necessary, beat in milk, 1 tablespoon at a time, to reach spreading consistency.
PER SERVING 638 cal., 31 g fat (19 g sat. fat), 89 mg chol., 591 mg sodium, 86 g carb., 2 g fiber, 6 g pro.

White Chocolate Curls Place 1½ ounces white chocolate (not baking pieces) and 1 teaspoon shortening in a small, heavy saucepan. Melt over low heat, stirring constantly. Use an offset metal spatula to evenly spread the chocolate in a glass baking dish. Let stand until set. Hold a straightedge metal spatula against the baking dish just inside the edge of the chocolate at a 45-degree angle. Apply gentle, steady pressure, and push the spatula straight forward. For looser curls, push spatula forward in an arc. Lift any curls with a wooden skewer to avoid making fingerprints in the chocolate. Use immediately or place a single layer on paper towels in a storage container. Cover and store at room temperature or chill.

Honey Vanilla Puffs

PREP 50 minutes COOL 10 minutes
BAKE 25 minutes at 375°F
MAKES 40 servings

- 1 cup water
- ¾ cup butter
- ½ cup whole milk
- 1 tablespoon honey
- 1 teaspoon vanilla bean paste
- ½ teaspoon salt
- 1½ cups all purpose flour
- 6 eggs
  Red decorating sugar
- 1 recipe Sweetened Whipped Cream (optional)

1. Preheat oven to 375°F. Line two baking sheets with parchment paper; set aside. In a large saucepan combine the water, butter, milk, honey, vanilla bean paste, and salt over medium heat, stirring until butter is melted and liquid just begins to simmer. Add the flour all at once and stir with a wooden spoon until the mixture becomes a very thick paste and pulls away from the sides of the saucepan. Continue stirring for 1 minute.
2. Remove and cool for 10 minutes. Add the eggs, one at a time, beating well with a wooden spoon after each addition. The dough should be a smooth, shiny paste.
3. Pipe or spoon about 2-inch mounds of dough about 1 inch apart on prepared baking sheets. Sprinkle generously with red sugar.
4. Bake for 25 minutes or until puffed and golden. Remove and cool on a wire rack. If desired, split and fill with Sweetened Whipped Cream.
PER SERVING 66 cal., 4 g fat (2 g sat. fat), 37 mg chol., 72 mg sodium, 5 g carb., 0 g fiber, 2 g pro.

Sweetened Whipped Cream Chill a medium bowl and beaters of a mixer in the freezer at least 30 minutes. In the chilled bowl combine 1 cup whipping cream and 2 tablespoons powdered sugar. Beat with a mixer on medium just until soft peaks form. Add ½ cup cold melted vanilla bean ice cream. Continue to beat until stiff peaks form (tips stand straight).

Vanilla Bean Soufflés with Quick Vanilla Custard Sauce

PREP 30 minutes
BAKE 30 minutes at 350°F
MAKES 6 servings

      Butter, softened
      Sugar
1¼ cups half-and-half, light cream, or whole milk
1   4- to 6-inch vanilla bean or 1 tablespoon vanilla
¼   cup butter
⅓   cup all-purpose flour
6   egg yolks, lightly beaten
6   egg whites
1   teaspoon vanilla
½   cup sugar
1   recipe Quick Vanilla Custard Sauce

1. Adjust the oven rack to the lowest position. Preheat oven to 350°F. Butter six 10-ounce custard cups or eight 6-ounce custard cups and sprinkle with sugar. To make collars for the soufflé dishes, measure enough foil to wrap around the top of each dish and add 3 inches. Fold the foil in thirds lengthwise. Lightly butter one side of the foil and sprinkle with sugar. Attach the foil, sugar side in, around the outside of the dish so the foil extends 2 inches above the dish. Tape or pin the ends of the foil together.
2. In a small saucepan heat half-and-half and vanilla bean (if using) until bubbles form at the edge of the saucepan. Remove from heat. Remove vanilla bean; cool 5 minutes. Using a paring knife, slit vanilla bean lengthwise. Scrape out seeds. Stir seeds (or the 1 tablespoon vanilla, if using) into half-in-half.
3. In another small saucepan melt the ¼ cup butter. Stir in the flour. Add half-and-half mixture. Whisk over medium heat until thickened and bubbly. Remove from heat (mixture will be thick). Gradually whisk the mixture into the beaten yolks.
4. In a large mixing bowl beat egg whites and the 1 teaspoon vanilla with a mixer on medium until soft peaks form (tips curl). Gradually add the ½ cup sugar, about 1 tablespoon at a time, beating on medium-high until stiff peaks form (tips stand straight).
5. Gently fold the egg yolk mixture into the egg white mixture. Spoon into the prepared soufflé dishes then place in a 15×10×1-inch baking pan. Bake for 30 minutes for 10-ounce dishes or 20 minutes for 6-ounce dishes, or until a knife inserted near center comes out clean. Serve immediately with Quick Vanilla Custard Sauce.

Quick Vanilla Custard Sauce Soften 1½ cups good-quality vanilla bean ice cream in the refrigerator for 3 hours or until pourable. Stir in ¼ teaspoon vanilla before serving over hot soufflés.

2-quart soufflé Butter the sides of a 2-quart soufflé dish and sprinkle with sugar. Make the collar as in Step 1. Bake for 40 to 45 minutes or until a knife inserted near center comes out clean.

PER SERVING 448 cal., 27 g fat (16 g sat. fat), 300 mg chol., 176 mg sodium, 39 g carb., 0 g fiber, 10 g pro.

VANILLA BEAN SOUFFLÉS WITH QUICK VANILLA CUSTARD SAUCE

Blueberry Bread Pudding with Blueberry Sauce

PREP 35 minutes
BAKE 50 minutes at 350°F
COOL 30 minutes MAKES 9 servings

5   cups dried French bread cubes
1   cup blueberries
½   cup chopped pecans, toasted (tip, page 32)
⅓   cup flaked coconut, toasted (tip, page 32)
2   eggs, lightly beaten
2¼ cups milk
½   cup granulated sugar
¼   cup butter, melted
1   tablespoon vanilla
¾   teaspoon ground cinnamon
¼   teaspoon ground nutmeg
      Blueberries (optional)
      Powdered sugar (optional)
1   recipe Blueberry Sauce

1. Preheat oven to 350°F. Spread bread cubes in an ungreased 2-quart square baking dish. Gently stir in 1 cup blueberries, the pecans, and coconut.
2. In a large bowl combine eggs, milk, granulated sugar, melted butter, vanilla, cinnamon, and nutmeg. Pour egg mixture over bread mixture. Press lightly with the back of a large spoon to moisten all the ingredients.
3. Bake for 50 minutes or until top is evenly puffed and a knife inserted in center comes out clean.
4. Cool on a wire rack for 30 to 45 minutes. If desired, top with additional blueberries and sprinkle lightly with powdered sugar. Serve warm with Blueberry Sauce.

Blueberry Sauce In a blender combine ½ cup blueberries and 2 tablespoons whipping cream. Cover and blend until blueberries are pureed. Strain through a fine-mesh sieve into a bowl, pressing berries with a spoon to release their juices. Stir 1½ cups powdered sugar, 1 teaspoon corn syrup, and ½ teaspoon vanilla into blueberry sauce. Stir in enough additional whipping cream, 1 teaspoon at a time, to reach drizzling consistency.

PER SERVING 379 cal., 15 g fat (6 g sat. fat), 67 mg chol., 230 mg sodium, 55 g carb., 2 g fiber, 7 g pro.

BLUEBERRY BREAD
PUDDING WITH
BLUEBERRY SAUCE

PEAR DUMPLINGS WITH
MAPLE-ORANGE SAUCE

Pear Dumplings with Maple-Orange Sauce

PREP 15 minutes
BAKE 18 minutes at 400°F
MAKES 4 servings

½ of a 15-ounce package (1 crust) rolled refrigerated unbaked piecrust
2 tablespoons chopped pecans or walnuts, toasted (tip, page 32)
2 tablespoons chopped pitted dates
1 teaspoon packed brown sugar
¼ teaspoon all-purpose flour
¼ teaspoon ground cinnamon
Dash salt
½ teaspoon butter, softened
2 medium Bosc pears
1 egg yolk
1 tablespoon water
Coarse sugar
1 recipe Maple-Orange Sauce

1. Preheat oven to 400°F. Line a baking sheet with parchment paper. Let piecrust stand according to package directions.
2. Meanwhile, for filling, in a small bowl combine pecans, dates, brown sugar, flour, cinnamon, and salt. Stir in softened butter until combined.
3. Peel pears. Cut in half lengthwise; remove stems. Using a melon baller or a measuring tablespoon, remove cores, scooping out tablespoon-size indentations. Spoon filling into indentations, packing lightly.
4. Unroll piecrust; cut into four wedges. For each dumpling, place a pear half, filling side up, on a wedge of pastry, positioning top of pear toward point of wedge. Lightly moisten edges of pastry with water. Fold sides of pastry over pear, then lightly mold pastry to enclose pear. Place dumplings, filling sides down, on the prepared baking sheet.
5. In a small bowl combine egg yolk and 1 tablespoon water; brush over dumplings; sprinkle with coarse sugar. If desired, cut small leaves from additional pastry and press onto pears. Bake for 18 to 22 minutes or until pastry is golden. Cool slightly. Serve warm with Maple-Orange Sauce.

ORANGE-GRAPEFRUIT COBBLER

Maple-Orange Sauce In a small saucepan combine ⅓ cup orange juice, ¼ cup maple syrup, ⅛ teaspoon cinnamon, and a pinch of ground allspice. Bring to boiling, reduce heat, and simmer 6 minutes or until reduced to ⅓ cup. Remove from heat, and whisk in 1 tablespoon chilled butter until completely incorporated. Serve sauce warm or at room temperature.
PER SERVING 448 cal., 21 g fat (8 g sat. fat), 55 mg chol., 290 mg sodium, 64 g carb., 5 g fiber, 3 g pro.

Orange-Grapefruit Cobbler

PREP 35 minutes
BAKE 20 minutes at 400°F
MAKES 9 servings

3 tablespoons sugar
1 tablespoon cornstarch
¼ teaspoon ground ginger
⅛ teaspoon ground nutmeg
¼ cup water
6 navel, Cara Cara, and/or blood oranges, peeled, seeded, and sectioned
2 pink or red grapefruit, peeled, seeded, and sectioned
1 cup all-purpose flour
1 tablespoon sugar
1½ teaspoons baking powder
¼ teaspoon ground ginger
⅛ teaspoon salt
2 tablespoons butter
⅓ cup plain low-fat yogurt
¼ cup refrigerated or frozen egg product, thawed, or 1 egg, lightly beaten
1 tablespoon fat-free milk
2 tablespoons flaked coconut, toasted (tip, page 32) (optional)
9 tablespoons frozen fat-free whipped dessert topping, thawed (optional)

1. Preheat oven to 400°F. For filling, in a medium saucepan stir together 3 tablespoons sugar, cornstarch, ¼ teaspoon ginger, and nutmeg. Stir in the water. Cook and stir over medium heat until thickened. Gently stir in orange sections and grapefruit sections. Keep the filling hot.
2. For cobbler, in a medium bowl stir together flour, 1 tablespoon sugar, baking powder, ¼ teaspoon ginger, and salt. Using a pastry blender, cut in butter until mixture resembles coarse crumbs. In a small bowl combine yogurt, egg, and milk. Add yogurt mixture to flour mixture, stirring just until moistened.
3. Spoon hot filling into an ungreased 2-quart square baking dish. Using two spoons, drop cobbler in nine mounds onto hot filling.
4. Bake for 20 to 25 minutes or until a wooden toothpick inserted in cobbler comes out clean. Serve warm. If desired, sprinkle with toasted coconut and/or top with dessert topping.
PER SERVING 172 cal., 3 g fat (2 g sat. fat), 7 mg chol., 111 mg sodium, 34 g carb., 3 g fiber, 4 g pro.

Oatmeal-Butterscotch Cookie Cheesecake

PREP 25 minutes STAND 30 minutes
BAKE 45 minutes at 350°F
COOL 2 hours CHILL 4 hours
MAKES 12 servings

3 8-ounce packages cream cheese
3 eggs, lightly beaten
2 cups rolled oats
½ cup broken pecans
2 tablespoons packed brown sugar
½ teaspoon ground cinnamon
½ cup butter, melted
½ cup granulated sugar
½ cup packed brown sugar
2 tablespoons all-purpose flour
1 teaspoon vanilla
½ teaspoon orange zest (optional)
¼ cup milk
1¼ cups butterscotch-flavor pieces

1. Allow cream cheese and eggs to stand at room temperature for 30 minutes. Meanwhile, preheat oven to 350°F. For crust, in a food processor combine oats, pecans, 2 tablespoons brown sugar, and cinnamon. Cover and pulse until oats and nuts are finely chopped. Add melted butter; cover and pulse just until combined. Remove ¼ cup of the oat mixture. Press the remaining oat mixture onto the bottom and about 1 inch up the sides of a 9-inch springform pan.
2. For filling, in a large mixing bowl beat cream cheese, granulated sugar, ½ cup brown sugar, flour, vanilla, and, if desired, orange peel with a mixer on medium until combined. Beat in milk until smooth. Stir in eggs and 1 cup of the butterscotch pieces.
3. Pour filling into crust-lined pan, spreading evenly. Sprinkle the reserved oat mixture and the remaining ¼ cup butterscotch pieces around edge. Place springform pan in a shallow baking pan.
4. Bake for 45 to 50 minutes or until a 2½-inch area around edge appears set when gently shaken. Cool in springform pan on a wire rack for 15 minutes. Using a small sharp knife, loosen crust from sides of pan. Cool for 30 minutes more. Remove sides of pan; cool cheesecake completely on wire rack. Cover and chill for at least 4 hours before serving.

PER SERVING 580 cal., 39 g fat (23 g sat. fat), 130 mg chol., 291 mg sodium, 50 g carb., 2 g fiber, 8 g pro.

OATMEAL-
BUTTERSCOTCH
COOKIE CHEESECAKE

S'more Pie a la Marshmallow Crème

PREP 45 minutes
COOL 20 minutes
CHILL 4 hours MAKES 10 servings

1 recipe Graham Cracker Crust
6 ounces bittersweet, semisweet, or milk chocolate, finely chopped
¼ cup water
¼ cup whipping cream
2 tablespoons dark-color corn syrup
2 teaspoons vanilla or crème de cacao
½ of a 8-ounce carton mascarpone cheese or ½ of an 8-ounce package cream cheese, softened (4 ounces)
1 cup whipping cream
½ cup powdered sugar
2 cups tiny marshmallows
1 7-ounce jar marshmallow creme
1 tablespoon crème de cacao or milk

1. Prepare the Graham Cracker Crust.
2. In a small heavy saucepan combine chocolate, the water, ¼ cup whipping cream, and corn syrup. Heat and stir constantly over medium-low heat until mixture is smooth and chocolate is melted. Remove from heat; stir in vanilla. Cool for 20 minutes; stirring occasionally.
3. For pie filling, in a medium bowl stir together the chocolate mixture and mascarpone; set aside. In a chilled metal mixing bowl beat the 1 cup whipping cream and powdered sugar with a mixer on medium, beating until soft peaks form (tips curl). Using a large spatula, gently fold whipped cream into the chocolate mixture.
4. Place 1 cup of the marshmallows in the baked crust. Spoon pie filling over marshmallows. Cover and chill at least 4 hours or until well chilled.
5. Meanwhile, for Marshmallow Creme, in a medium bowl combine marshmallow creme and creme de cacao. Stir in remaining marshmallows.
6. If desired, brown marshmallows in Marshmallow Crème with a kitchen torch. Cut pie into wedges and serve with Marshmallow Crème.

Graham Cracker Crust Lightly coat a 9-inch pie plate with cooking spray. In a medium saucepan melt ⅓ cup butter over medium heat; remove from heat. Stir in ¼ cup sugar. Add 1¼ cups finely crushed graham crackers (about 18). Spread in the prepared pie plate; press evenly onto bottom and sides. Bake in a 375°F oven 5 minutes or until edges are light brown. Cool completely on a wire rack before filling.

PER SERVING 511 cal., 30 g fat (18 g sat. fat), 72 mg chol., 167 mg sodium, 61 g carb., 2 g fiber, 5 g pro.

S'MORE PIE A LA MARSHMALLOW CRÈME

TRIPLE-PEAR PIE
WITH WALNUT
CRUST

Triple-Pear Pie with Walnut Crust

PREP 45 minutes
BAKE 1 hour 20 minutes at 375°F
MAKES 8 servings

⅓ cup walnuts, toasted (tip, page 32)
2 tablespoons packed brown sugar
1 teaspoon salt
2½ cups all-purpose flour
½ cup cold unsalted butter, cut up
¼ cup shortening, chilled and cut up
⅓ to ½ cup ice water
⅔ cup pear nectar or apple juice
¾ cup chopped dried pears or golden raisins
½ teaspoon ground cardamom
¼ teaspoon ground nutmeg
½ cup packed brown sugar
3 tablespoons all-purpose flour
8 ripe Bosc pears
1 egg, lightly beaten
2 teaspoons water
Coarse white decorating sugar

1. Preheat oven to 375°F. In a food processor combine the walnuts, 2 tablespoons brown sugar, and salt; pulse until walnuts are finely ground. Add 2½ cups flour and pulse until combined. Add cold butter and shortening and pulse until mixture resembles coarse crumbs. Drizzle the ice cold water, about 1 tablespoon at a time, through feed tube while pulsing just until mixture begins to come together (do not overprocess). Dough should be slightly crumbly, and come together with your hands when gently squeezed. Gather dough into a ball, divide it in half, and shape each half into a disk. Wrap disks in plastic wrap and chill while preparing pie filling.
2. In a small saucepan bring pear nectar to a simmer over medium-high heat. Add dried pears, cardamom, and nutmeg; remove from heat and set aside.
3. For filling, in a large bowl combine ½ cup brown sugar and 3 tablespoons flour. Peel, core, and slice pears ½ inch thick; add to sugar mixture in bowl. Toss pears to coat with sugar mixture. Add undrained dried pear mixture and toss to combine.
4. On a lightly floured surface roll out one disk of dough into a 12-inch

PECAN PIE SLABS

circle. Ease pastry into a 9-inch pie plate, allowing pastry to extend over edge. In a small bowl combine egg and 2 teaspoons water. Lightly brush pastry with some of the egg mixture. Spoon filling evenly into pastry-lined pie plate. Trim pastry to edge of pie plate.
5. Roll out remaining pastry on the floured surface to an 11-inch circle. Cut slits in top pastry and place over filling. Fold top pastry under bottom pastry and crimp edges to seal. Brush with egg mixture and sprinkle with coarse sugar.
6. Loosely cover pie with foil to prevent overbrowning. Bake for 50 minutes. Remove foil and bake for 30 to 40 minutes more or until pastry is golden, pears are tender, and filling is bubbly (if necessary, cover with foil the last 10 minutes of baking to prevent overbrowning.) Cool on a wire rack.

PER SERVING 563 cal., 22 g fat (9 g sat. fat), 54 mg chol., 310 mg sodium, 85 g carb., 8 g fiber, 7 g pro.

Pecan Pie Slabs

PREP 25 minutes
BAKE 40 minutes at 350°F
MAKES 24 servings

1¼ cups all-purpose flour
½ cup powdered sugar
¼ teaspoon salt
½ cup butter
2 eggs, slightly beaten
1 cup chopped pecans
½ cup packed brown sugar
½ cup light-color corn syrup
2 tablespoons butter, melted
1 teaspoon vanilla

1. Preheat oven to 350°F. Line an 11×7×1½-inch baking pan with foil, extending foil over the edges of pan.
2. For crust, in a medium bowl stir together flour, powdered sugar, and salt. Using a pastry blender, cut in the ½ cup butter until mixture resembles coarse crumbs. Pat crumb mixture into the prepared baking pan. Bake for 20 minutes or until light brown.
3. Meanwhile, for filling, in a medium bowl stir together eggs, pecans, brown sugar, corn syrup, the 2 tablespoons melted butter, and vanilla. Pour over the baked crust, spreading evenly. Bake for 20 minutes more or until the filling is set. Cool completely in pan on a wire rack.
4. Use foil to lift out of pan. Cut into slabs.

PER SERVING 150 cal., 9 g fat (3 g sat. fat), 31 mg chol., 76 mg sodium, 17 g carb., 1 g fiber, 2 g pro.

HONEYCRISP APPLE
AND BROWNED-
BUTTER TART

Honeycrisp Apple and Browned-Butter Tart

PREP 45 minutes BAKE 13 minutes
at 450°F/35 minutes at 350°F
COOL 1 hour MAKES 12 servings

  1 recipe Pâte Sucrée
  2 tablespoons butter
  ½ cup sugar
  5 large Honeycrisp apples, cored
     and each cut into 8 wedges
     (3½ pounds)
  ½ cup butter
  3 egg yolks
  ⅓ cup sugar
  ¼ teaspoon salt
  ¼ teaspoon almond extract
  ⅓ cup all-purpose flour
     Vanilla ice cream (optional)

1. Prepare Pâte Sucrée. Preheat oven to 450°F. On a lightly floured surface use your hands to slightly flatten Pâte Sucrée pastry. Roll pastry from center to edges into a circle about 12 inches in diameter. Wrap pastry circle around rolling pin. Unroll into a 10-inch tart pan with a removable bottom. Ease pastry into tart pan without stretching it. Press pastry into fluted sides of tart pan; trim edges. Line pastry with a double thickness of foil. Bake for 8 minutes. Remove foil. Bake for 5 minutes more or until golden. Cool on a wire rack. Reduce oven temperature to 350°F.

2. In a large skillet heat 2 tablespoons butter over medium heat until melted. Stir in ½ cup sugar. Cook and stir until mixture begins to brown. Add apple wedges. Cook and stir for 10 to 12 minutes or until apples are light golden brown. Set aside.

3. For browned butter, in a small saucepan heat ½ cup butter over medium heat until melted. Reduce heat to medium-low. Continue cooking, without stirring, for 5 to 6 minutes or until butter turns a light golden brown.

4. For custard filling, in a medium mixing bowl beat egg yolks, ⅓ cup sugar, salt, and almond extract with a mixer on medium until thickened. Beat in flour on low until combined. Add browned butter, beating on low just until combined.

5. Pour filling into baked crust, spreading evenly. Using a slotted spoon, remove apple wedges from skillet and arrange on filling. Drizzle apples with any cooking liquid remaining in skillet. Cover edge of tart with foil. Bake for 35 to 45 minutes or until custard filling is puffed and set in the center. Cool on a wire rack about 1 hour to serve warm, or cool completely. Remove sides of tart pan. Cover and chill within 2 hours. If desired, serve with vanilla ice cream.

Pâte Sucrée In a food processor combine 1¼ cups flour and 2 tablespoons sugar. Cover and process just until combined. Add ½ cup butter, cut up. Cover and pulse until pieces are pea size. In a small bowl combine 2 tablespoons whipping cream and 1 egg yolk, lightly beaten. Add the cream mixture through the feed tube. Stop food processor as soon as the mixture is added; scrape down side. Pulse twice (dough may not be all moistened). Remove dough from the bowl; shape into a disk. If necessary, cover and chill for 1 hour or until dough is easy to handle.

PER SERVING *364 cal., 20 g fat (12 g sat. fat), 119 mg chol., 176 mg sodium, 45 g carb., 3 g fiber, 3 g pro.*

Caramel Pecan Skillet Brownie

PREP **25 minutes**
BAKE **35 minutes at 325°F**
COOL **15 minutes** MAKES **10 servings**

1⅓ cups packed brown sugar
1 cup all-purpose flour
½ cup unsweetened cocoa powder
2 teaspoons instant coffee crystals
¾ teaspoon baking soda
½ teaspoon salt
1 cup coarsely chopped pecans
¼ cup butter
½ cup packed brown sugar
½ cup whipping cream
6 tablespoons butter, melted
4 eggs, lightly beaten
¼ cup whipping cream
6 ounces dark chocolate, coarsely chopped
Coffee or vanilla ice cream (optional)

1. Preheat oven to 325°F. In a medium mixing bowl combine the 1⅓ cups brown sugar, the flour, cocoa powder, coffee crystals, baking soda, and salt.
2. Heat a 10×2-inch cast-iron or other heavy ovensafe skillet over medium-high heat. Add pecans; cook and stir for 2 to 3 minutes or until lightly toasted. Add ¼ cup butter to skillet; stir to melt, then add ½ cup brown sugar to skillet. Cook, stirring constantly, until mixture bubbles and brown sugar begins to melt.
3. Remove skillet from heat and carefully add ½ cup cream to skillet. Return to heat; cook until sugar is melted.
4. Add 6 tablespoons melted butter, eggs, and ¼ cup cream to flour and cocoa mixture in bowl; stir until combined. Fold in chopped dark chocolate. Carefully spoon batter over nuts in skillet.
5. Bake for 35 minutes or just until set (place a shallow baking pan on the rack below to catch any drips). Remove from oven and cool slightly on a wire rack. If desired, serve warm with ice cream.

PER SERVING *573 cal., 34 g fat (13 g sat. fat), 130 mg chol., 361 mg sodium, 64 g carb., 4 g fiber, 7 g pro.*

CARAMEL PECAN
SKILLET BROWNIE

Bake and Share

THE CHRISTMAS SEASON truly arrives when platters of homemade cookies begin to be filled and shared with family and friends. Seek inspiration for this season's exchange with this collection of dropped, rolled, shaped, filled, and whimsically decorated treats.

GINGERBREAD
VILLAGE, PAGE 96

Almond Wreath Cookies

PREP 40 minutes
BAKE 16 minutes at 350°F
MAKES 24 servings

  2 8-ounce cans almond paste
  ⅔ cup granulated sugar
  ½ teaspoon salt
  3 egg whites, lightly beaten
  ½ cup all-purpose flour
  1 cup sliced almonds
     Granulated sugar

1. Preheat oven to 350°F. Line cookie sheets with parchment paper; set aside. Crumble almond paste into a large mixing bowl. Add ⅔ cup sugar, salt, and two of the egg whites; beat with a mixer on medium until a thick, sticky paste forms.
2. Sprinkle flour over a work surface. Knead dough into flour. Roll dough out on a lightly floured surface to ½-inch thickness. Use a floured doughnut cutter to cut wreath shapes. Reroll scraps as necessary.
3. Arrange cutouts 1 inch apart on cookie sheets. Brush with remaining egg white. Arrange almond slices and sprinkles on top. Brush almonds with egg white and sprinkle with additional sugar.
4. Bake for 16 to 18 minutes or until golden brown. Cool on wire racks.
PER SERVING *148 cal., 7 g fat (1 g sat. fat), 0 mg chol., 57 mg sodium, 19 g carb., 1 g fiber, 3 g pro.*

Cinnamon-Almond Slices

PREP 25 minutes CHILL 2 hours
BAKE 8 minutes at 350°F
MAKES 64 servings

  ⅔ cup butter, softened
  1 8-ounce can almond paste
  ¼ cup packed brown sugar
  1 teaspoon baking powder
  1 teaspoon ground cinnamon
  ½ teaspoon salt
  1 egg
  2 cups all-purpose flour
  ¼ cup toasted almonds, finely chopped (tip, page 32)

1. In a large mixing bowl beat butter with a mixer on medium to high for 30 seconds. Add almond paste, brown sugar, baking powder, cinnamon, and salt. Beat until combined, scraping sides of bowl occasionally. Beat in egg until combined. Beat in as much of the flour as you can with the mixer. Stir in remaining flour and the almonds.
2. Divide dough in half. Shape each half into an 8-inch roll. Wrap each roll in plastic wrap or waxed paper. Chill for 2 hours or until dough is firm enough to slice.
3. Preheat oven to 350°F. If necessary, reshape rolls to make them round. Using a serrated knife, cut rolls into ¼-inch slices. Place slices 1 inch apart on an ungreased cookie sheet.
4. Bake for 8 to 10 minutes or until edges are firm and centers are set. Cool on wire racks.
PER SERVING *72 cal., 4 g fat (2 g sat. fat), 11 mg chol., 59 mg sodium, 8 g carb., 0 g fiber, 1 g pro.*

CINNAMON-ALMOND SLICES

Coconut Spritz Cookies

PREP **1 hour**
BAKE **10 minutes at 325°F**
MAKES **72 servings**

- 2 cups unsalted butter, softened
- 1 cup granulated sugar
- 2 eggs
- ½ cup unsweetened coconut milk
- 3½ cups all-purpose flour
- 1 cup sweetened shredded coconut, finely chopped in a food processor
- 1 teaspoon salt
- ½ teaspoon baking powder
  Powdered sugar

1. Preheat oven to 325°F. Line baking sheets with parchment paper. Trace 2½- to 3-inch circles 1 inch apart on the parchment. Flip parchment over.
2. In a large bowl beat butter and sugar with a mixer on medium to high until light and fluffy. Add the eggs, one at a time, beating on low after each addition. Beat in the coconut milk. In a medium bowl whisk together the flour, coconut, salt, and baking powder. Add to butter mixture; beat on low until combined.
3. Transfer dough to a pastry bag fitted with a ¼-inch open star or round tip. Pipe small loops around each drawn circle. Bake for 10 to 12 minutes or until edges just begin to brown. Cool completely on baking sheets. Sprinkle with powdered sugar.
PER SERVING *88 cal., 6 g fat (4 g sat. fat), 19 mg chol., 42 mg sodium, 8 g carb., 0 g fiber, 1 g pro.*

Maple-Macadamia Icebox Cookies

PREP **30 minutes** CHILL **2 hours**
BAKE **10 minutes at 325°F**
MAKES **60 servings**

- 1 cup butter, softened
- ¾ cup maple sugar or packed brown sugar plus ¼ teaspoon maple flavoring
- ½ cup powdered sugar
- ½ teaspoon salt
- ¼ teaspoon ground cinnamon
- 2 egg yolks
- 2 teaspoons vanilla
- 2¼ cups all-purpose flour
- ¼ cup finely chopped macadamia nuts
- 1 recipe Maple Glaze

1. In a large mixing bowl beat butter with a mixer on medium to high for 30 seconds. Add maple sugar, powdered sugar, salt, and cinnamon. Beat until combined, scraping bowl occasionally. Beat in egg yolks and vanilla until combined. Beat in as much of the flour as you can with the mixer. Stir in remaining flour and macadamia nuts.
2. Divide dough in half. Shape each half into a 10-inch roll. Wrap each roll in plastic wrap. Chill dough for 2 hours or until firm enough to slice.
3. Preheat oven to 325°F. Cut rolls into ¼-inch slices. Place slices 1 inch apart on an ungreased cookie sheet.
4. Bake for 10 to 12 minutes or just until edges are firm and tops start to brown. Cool on cookie sheet 1 minute. Transfer cookies to a wire rack; cool.
5. Drizzle cookies with Maple Glaze. Let stand until glaze is set.
Maple Glaze In a medium bowl stir together 1½ cups powdered sugar and ¼ cup maple syrup. Stir in 1 to 2 tablespoons milk to make drizzling consistency.
PER SERVING *76 cal., 4 g fat (2 g sat. fat), 14 mg chol., 47 mg sodium, 10 g carb., 0 g fiber, 1 g pro.*

Reindeer Palmiers

PREP 10 minutes   CHILL 4 hours
BAKE 15 minutes at 400°F
MAKES 38 servings

½ cup turbinado (raw) sugar
½ teaspoon ground ginger
¼ teaspoon ground cinnamon
  Pinch ground nutmeg
1 17.3-ounce package (2 sheets) frozen puff pastry sheets, thawed
1 recipe Royal Icing
  Semisweet chocolate pieces and/or round red candies

1. In a small bowl stir together the sugar, ginger, cinnamon, and nutmeg. Spread half the sugar mixture onto a piece of parchment paper. Unfold one puff pastry sheet and place on sugar mixture. Roll pastry to a 12×10-inch rectangle. (Dust top of pastry with flour to prevent sticking to rolling pin.) Roll the short sides of pastry toward each other to meet in the center. Wrap in plastic wrap and chill for 4 to 24 hours. (Or freeze for 1 hour.) Return excess sugar mixture from parchment to bowl. Roll remaining pastry and half the sugar mixture.

2. Preheat oven to 400°F. Line two baking sheets with parchment paper. Slice the puff pastry roll crosswise into ½-inch slices. Dip the cut sides in reserved sugar mixture. Place 2 inches apart on prepared baking sheets, sugar side up. Gently unroll both sides of the pastry and pinch in center to form the nose.

3. Bake for 15 to 17 minutes or until golden. Cool on wire rack. Carefully peel cookies off parchment paper. To decorate, use Royal Icing dots for eyes and attach semisweet chocolate pieces with Royal Icing for nose.

Royal Icing In a bowl combine 1 cup powdered sugar and 1 teaspoon dried egg whites. Add 2 tablespoons water, 1 tablespoon at a time, until smooth.

PER SERVING *93 cal., 5 g fat (1 g sat. fat), 0 mg chol., 33 mg sodium, 11 g carb., 0 g fiber, 1 g pro.*

Gingerbread Village

PREP 35 minutes   CHILL 3 hours
BAKE 6 minutes at 375°F
MAKES 5 servings

¼ cup shortening
¼ cup granulated sugar
½ teaspoon baking powder
½ teaspoon ground ginger
¼ teaspoon baking soda
¼ teaspoon ground cinnamon
¼ cup molasses
1 egg yolk
1½ teaspoons vinegar
1¼ cups all-purpose flour
1 recipe Royal Icing (recipe left)
  Assorted sprinkles, jelly wreaths, and candies
  Bite-size shredded wheat and graham crackers

1. In a large mixing bowl beat shortening with a mixer on medium to high for 30 seconds. Add granulated sugar, baking powder, ginger, baking soda, and cinnamon. Beat until combined, scraping sides of bowl occasionally. Beat in molasses, egg yolk, and vinegar until combined. Beat in as much of the flour as you can. Stir in remaining flour. Divide dough in half. Cover; chill for 3 hours or until dough is easy to handle.

2. Preheat oven to 375°F. Grease cookie sheets; set aside. On a lightly floured surface roll half the dough at a time to ⅛- to ¼-inch thickness. Using 4- to 6-inch house-shape cookie cutters and/or 2- to 3-inch gingerbread people cookie cutters, cut out dough. Place house cutouts and/or gingerbread people cutouts on separate prepared cookie sheets. If desired, use a table knife to cut out windows and doors in house.

3. Bake until edges are lightly browned. Allow 6 minutes for gingerbread people and 8 minutes for houses. Cool on cookie sheets for 1 minute. Transfer cookies to a wire rack to cool.

4. Decorate cookies with icing, candies, and crackers.

PER SERVING *82 cal., 3 g fat (1 g sat. fat), 6 mg chol., 28 mg sodium, 13 g carb., 0 g fiber, 1 g pro.*

REINDEER PALMIERS

ENGLISH LEMON
CURD SANDWICH
COOKIES

Lemon Curd In a medium saucepan stir together 1 cup sugar and 2 tablespoons cornstarch. Stir in 1 tablespoon finely shredded lemon peel, 6 tablespoons lemon juice, and 6 tablespoons water. Cook and stir over medium heat until thickened and bubbly. Stir half the lemon mixture into 6 beaten egg yolks. Return egg mixture to the saucepan. Cook, stirring constantly, over medium heat until mixture comes to a gentle boil. Cook and stir for 2 minutes more. Remove from heat. Add ½ cup cut-up butter pieces, stirring until melted. Cover surface of curd with plastic wrap. Chill at least 1 hour or up to 48 hours. Store covered in refrigerator up to 1 week or transfer to a freezer container and freeze up to 2 months. Thaw in refrigerator before serving. Makes about 2 cups.

PER SERVING   126 cal., 8 g fat (4 g sat. fat), 42 mg chol., 91 mg sodium, 13 g carb., 0 g fiber, 1 g pro.

Orange-Cream Cheese Sugar Cookie Snowmen

PREP 30 minutes   CHILL 1 hour
BAKE 7 minutes at 350°F
MAKES 36 servings

    ½ cup sugar
    2 teaspoons orange or lemon zest
    ⅔ cup butter, softened
    3 ounces cream cheese, softened
    ½ teaspoon baking powder
    ¼ teaspoon salt
    3 tablespoons milk
    1 teaspoon vanilla
   2¼ cups all-purpose flour
       White icing or frosting
       Shredded coconut
       Pretzel sticks, sixlets candy,
       airhead ribbons, and mini
       chocolate chips

1. In a small bowl combine sugar and orange zest. Press the zest into sugar with the back of a spoon until the sugar is fragrant and begins to turn orange; set aside.
2. In a large mixing bowl beat butter and cream cheese with a mixer on medium to high for 30 seconds. Add sugar mixture, baking powder, and

English Lemon Curd Sandwich Cookies

PREP 30 minutes   CHILL 1 hour
BAKE 12 minutes at 350°F
MAKES 48 servings

   2½ cups all-purpose flour
    ½ teaspoon baking soda
    ½ teaspoon salt
    1 cup butter, softened
    ¾ cup granulated sugar
    1 egg
    1 teaspoon vanilla
    1 cup finely ground pecans
    1 recipe Lemon Curd or 2 cups
       purchased lemon curd

1. In a medium bowl stir together flour, baking soda, and salt; set aside. In a large mixing bowl beat butter with a mixer on medium to high for 30 seconds. Add sugar. Beat until

combined, scraping sides of bowl occasionally. Beat in egg and vanilla until combined. Beat in pecans and as much of the flour mixture as you can. Stir in remaining flour mixture. Divide dough in half. Cover and chill about 1 hour or until dough is easy to handle.
2. Preheat oven to 350°F. On a lightly floured surface roll half the dough at a time to ⅛-inch thickness. Using a floured 2-inch scalloped round cookie cutter, cut out dough. Place cutouts 1 inch apart on an ungreased cookie sheet. Using a ½-inch round cookie cutter, cut and remove a circle from the center of half the cookies.
3. Bake for 12 to 15 minutes or until lightly browned. Transfer cookies to a wire rack; cool.
4. Spread 1½ teaspoons Lemon Curd on bottoms of cookies without cutout centers. Top with cookies with cutout centers, bottom sides down.

ORANGE-CREAM CHEESE SUGAR COOKIE SNOWMEN

salt. Beat until combined, scraping sides of bowl occasionally. Beat in milk and vanilla until combined. Beat in as much of the flour as you can Stir in remaining flour. Divide dough in half. Cover and chill about 1 hour or until dough is easy to handle.

3. Preheat oven to 350°F. On a lightly floured surface roll one portion of dough at a time to ⅛-inch thickness.

Use three graduated sizes of round cookie cutters to cut a top, middle, and bottom for each snowman. For each snowman, on an ungreased cookie sheet slightly overlap three dough circles, spacing cookies 1 inch apart.

4. Bake for 7 to 9 minutes or until tops are set. Transfer cookies to a wire rack; cool completely.

5. Lightly spread white icing or frosting on each cookie; sprinkle with shredded coconut. Use pretzel sticks for arms, sixlets for buttons, airhead ribbons for scarves, and mini chocolate chips for eyes and mouth.

PER SERVING *79 cal., 4 g fat (3 g sat. fat), 12 mg chol., 61 mg sodium, 9 g carb., 0 g fiber, 1 g pro.*

Malted Chocolate Baubles

PREP 45 minutes
BAKE 12 minutes at 350°F
MAKES 24 servings

Nonstick cooking spray for baking
1 cup all-purpose flour
¼ cup vanilla malted milk powder
¼ cup unsweetened cocoa powder
½ teaspoon baking powder
½ teaspoon salt
½ teaspoon instant espresso coffee powder
½ cup milk
½ teaspoon white vinegar
½ teaspoon vanilla
¼ cup butter, softened
⅔ cup granulated sugar
1 egg
½ cup heavy cream
8 ounces good quality white baking chocolate or white baking pieces
1 to 2 drops red gel food coloring
Powdered sugar

1. Preheat oven to 350°F. For the baubles, spray a 12-cup cake-pop pan with nonstick baking spray then place on a baking sheet.
2. In a medium mixing bowl combine the flour, malted milk powder, cocoa, baking powder, salt, and instant espresso coffee powder. Whisk for 30 seconds to distribute the leavening. Set aside. Measure out the milk then add the vinegar and vanilla. Stir and let stand.
3. In a large mixing bowl beat the butter and granulated sugar with a mixer on medium to high until light and fluffy. Add the egg, beating until combined. Alternately add the flour mixture and milk mixture to the butter mixture, adding about half with each addition. Beat until smooth after each addition.
4. Add a slightly rounded tablespoon of batter to each bottom cavity of the prepared cake ball pan. Add the top according to manufacturer's directions. Bake for 12 to 15 minutes or until a toothpick inserted into the cake comes out clean. Cool 5 minutes on a wire rack. Remove cakes from pan. Cool completely.
5. For the ganache, in a small saucepan bring cream just to simmering. Remove from heat. Add white baking pieces. Let stand 5 minutes (do not stir). Stir until smooth. Stir in food coloring. Let stand or chill until firm enough to spread.
6. Split each cake and spread ganache on bottoms of each. Add tops. Dust with powdered sugar.

PER SERVING *150 cal., 8 g fat (5 g sat. fat), 23 mg chol., 104 mg sodium, 19 g carb., 0 g fiber, 2 g pro.*

MALTED CHOCOLATE BAUBLES

Frosted Blood Orange Cookies

PREP 1 hour CHILL 1 hour
BAKE 10 minutes at 350°F
MAKES 48 servings

1 cup butter, softened
¾ cup granulated sugar
1 tablespoon baking powder
¼ teaspoon salt
1 egg
2 teaspoons blood orange zest or orange zest
1 tablespoon blood orange juice or orange juice
¼ teaspoon anise extract

3 cups all-purpose flour
1 recipe Blood Orange Frosting
1 recipe Candied Citrus Threads

1. In a large mixing bowl beat butter with a mixer on medium to high for 30 seconds. Add sugar, baking powder, and salt. Beat until combined, scraping sides of bowl occasionally. Beat in egg, orange zest, orange juice, and anise extract until combined. Beat in as much of the flour as you can. Stir in remaining flour. Cover and chill about 1 hour or until dough is easy to handle.
2. Preheat oven to 350°F. Line a cookie sheet with parchment paper. Shape dough into 1-inch balls. Place balls 1 inch apart on the prepared cookie sheet. If desired, flatten balls to about ½ inch thick.
3. Bake for 10 minutes or until bottoms are lightly browned. Transfer cookies to a wire rack; cool. Spread tops of cookies with Blood Orange Frosting. Sprinkle with Candied Citrus Threads.

Blood Orange Frosting In a medium mixing bowl beat ¼ cup softened butter with a mixer on medium until smooth. Gradually add about 1½ cups powdered sugar, beating well. Beat in 3 tablespoons milk, 1 tablespoon orange zest, and ½ teaspoon vanilla. Beat in another 1½ cups powdered sugar. If necessary, beat in 1 tablespoon milk, 1 teaspoon at a time, to reach spreading consistency. Makes 1½ cups.

Candied Citrus Threads Using a citrus zester, remove blood orange peel in threadlike pieces from two blood oranges or oranges. In a small saucepan combine zest and enough water to cover. Bring just to boiling over medium-high heat; reduce heat. Simmer for 5 minutes; drain. In the same saucepan combine 1½ cups sugar and the 1½ cups water. Bring just to boiling over medium-high heat, stirring to dissolve sugar. Stir in zest; reduce heat. Simmer for 8 to 10 minutes or until zest is tender; drain well. Sprinkle a large shallow pan with enough sugar to cover lightly. Sprinkle zest evenly over sugar. Let stand until dry and brittle.

PER SERVING 119 cal., 5 g fat (3 g sat. fat), 17 mg chol., 87 mg sodium, 18 g carb., 0 g fiber, 1 g pro.

FROSTED BLOOD ORANGE COOKIES

VANILLA HOLIDAY
COOKIES

Vanilla Holiday Cookies

PREP 25 minutes FREEZE 1 hour
BAKE 8 minutes at 375°F
MAKES 24 servings

- ¾ cup (1½ sticks) unsalted butter, softened
- ½ cup sugar
- ½ teaspoon fine sea salt
- 2½ teaspoons vanilla
- 2 cups all-purpose flour
   Royal Icing
   Powdered Sugar Icing
   Assorted decors and sugars

1. Line two cookie sheets with parchment paper. In a large mixing bowl beat the butter, sugar, and salt with a mixer on medium-low until smooth, about 1 minute. Reduce speed to low; beat in vanilla. Turn off the mixer, add the flour all at once. With the mixer on low, beat just until the flour disappears into dough (dough may appear crumbly). Using your hands, work dough into a ball; divide in half.

2. Working with one dough piece at a time, roll between sheets of waxed paper to ¼-inch thickness. Freeze between the paper for 1 hour or until easy to handle.

3. Preheat oven to 375°F. Working with one dough piece at a time let stand at room temperature for 5 minutes. Using a 2-inch cutter, cut into shapes. Place 1 inch apart on cookie sheets. Gather scraps; repeat rolling and freezing, if necessary, between waxed paper.

4. Bake one cookie sheet at a time for 8 to 10 minutes or until cookies feel almost firm to the touch and are golden on the bottom and around the sides. Cool completely on wire racks.

5. To decorate, use thinned Royal Icing for the base coat of the cookies, and thickened Royal Icing for piping Santa's coat and stocking. For mitten and hat, pipe a second and/or third color of icing over the base coat while wet. Use a toothpick to drag through the colors.

Royal Icing In a large mixing bowl stir together one 16-ounce package powdered sugar, 3 tablespoons meringue powder, and ½ teaspoon cream of tartar. Add ½ cup warm water and 1 teaspoon vanilla. Beat with a mixer on low until combined; beat on high for 7 to 10 minutes or until icing reaches stiff piping consistency. If not using right away, cover bowl with a damp paper towel and cover paper towel with plastic wrap; chill for up to 48 hours.

Powdered Sugar Icing In a small bowl stir together 3 cups powdered sugar, 2 tablespoons milk, and ½ teaspoon vanilla or almond extract. If necessary, stir in additional milk, 1 teaspoon at a time, to reach drizzling consistency. Makes about 1 cup.

PER SERVING 106 cal., 6 g fat (4 g sat. fat), 15 mg chol., 47 mg sodium, 12 g carb., 0 g fiber, 1 g pro.

Soft S'more Cookies

PREP 25 minutes
BAKE 9 minutes at 350°F
MAKES 32 servings

- 1 16.5- or 18-ounce roll refrigerated chocolate chip cookie dough
- ½ cup finely crushed graham crackers
- 16 marshmallows, halved crosswise
- 2½ 1.55-ounce bars milk chocolate, divided into 32 pieces total
   Finely crushed graham crackers

1. Preheat oven to 350°F. In a large bowl stir together cookie dough and the ½ cup crushed graham crackers. Shape dough into thirty-two about 1-inch balls. Place balls 2 inches apart on an ungreased cookie sheet. Bake for 8 minutes.

2. Press a marshmallow half, cut side up, into the center of each cookie. Top with a piece of chocolate. Bake for 1 to 2 minutes more or until marshmallows are softened.

3. Immediately sprinkle cookies with additional crushed graham crackers. Serve warm or cool on a wire rack.

PER SERVING 100 cal., 4 g fat (2 g sat. fat), 2 mg chol., 62 mg sodium, 15 g carb., 0 g fiber, 1 g pro.

SOFT S'MORE COOKIES

**CHOCOLATE-CHERRY
THUMBPRINTS**

Chocolate-Cherry Thumbprints

PREP **30 minutes**
BAKE **10 minutes at 350°F**
MAKES **42 servings**

    2 cups frozen pitted dark sweet
       cherries (about 42)
    ½ cup butter, softened
    1 cup sugar
    ¼ teaspoon baking powder
    ¼ teaspoon baking soda
    ¼ teaspoon salt
    1 egg
   1½ teaspoons vanilla
    ½ cup unsweetened cocoa powder
   1½ cups all-purpose flour
    1 cup milk chocolate pieces
    ½ cup sweetened condensed milk
    4 teaspoons cherry liqueur or milk

1. Thaw cherries; pat dry with paper
towels. Set aside. Preheat oven to
350°F. In a medium mixing bowl beat
butter with a mixer on medium to
high for 30 seconds. Add sugar, baking
powder, baking soda, and salt. Beat
until combined, scraping sides of bowl
occasionally. Beat in egg and vanilla
until combined. Beat in cocoa powder
and as much of the flour as you can.
Stir in remaining flour.
2. Shape dough into 1-inch balls.
Place balls about 2 inches apart on an
ungreased cookie sheet. Press your
thumb into the center of each ball.
Place a cherry in each indentation.
3. For frosting, in a small saucepan
stir chocolate pieces and sweetened
condensed milk over low heat until
chocolate is melted. Stir in cherry
liqueur. Spoon about 1 teaspoon
frosting over each cherry.
4. Bake for 10 minutes or until edges
are firm. Cool on cookie sheet for
1 minute. Transfer cookies to a wire
rack; cool.
PER SERVING *103 cal., 5 g fat
(3 g sat. fat), 13 mg chol., 54 mg sodium,
15 g carb., 1 g fiber, 2 g pro.*

MOLASSES CRINKLES

Molasses Crinkles

PREP 20 minutes
BAKE 10 minutes at 375°F
MAKES 30 servings

¾ cup shortening
 1 cup packed brown sugar
 1 teaspoon baking soda
 1 teaspoon ground cinnamon
 1 teaspoon ground ginger
 ¼ teaspoon salt
 ¼ teaspoon ground cloves
 1 egg
 ¼ cup mild-flavor molasses
2¼ cups all-purpose flour
 ¼ cup coarse sugar

1. Preheat oven to 375°F. In a large bowl beat shortening with a mixer on medium to high for 30 seconds. Add brown sugar, baking soda, cinnamon, ginger, salt, and cloves. Beat until combined, scraping sides of bowl occasionally. Beat in egg and molasses until combined. Beat in as much of the flour as you can. Stir in any remaining flour. If necessary, cover and chill dough for 30 to 60 minutes or until easy to handle.
2. Place coarse sugar in a bowl. Shape dough into 1½-inch balls. Roll balls in coarse sugar to coat.
3. Place balls about 2 inches apart on an ungreased cookie sheet. Bake for 10 minutes or until edges are set and tops are crackled. Cool on wire racks.
PER SERVING *123 cal., 5 g fat (1 g sat. fat), 6 mg chol., 67 mg sodium, 18 g carb., 0 g fiber, 1 g pro.*

White Chocolate and Cherry Biscotti

PREP 35 minutes
BAKE 41 minutes at 325°F
COOL 45 minutes
MAKES 45 servings

 2 cups all-purpose flour
 1 cup sugar
 ¾ cup regular or quick-cooking rolled oats
 ½ cup cold butter, cut up
2½ teaspoons baking powder
 ½ teaspoon salt
 2 eggs, lightly beaten
 2 tablespoons cherry brandy, unsweetened cherry juice, or milk
 2 teaspoons vanilla
1¼ cups chopped toasted almonds (tip, page 32)
 ¾ cup snipped dried cherries
 4 ounces white baking chocolate with cocoa butter, chopped
 ¾ teaspoon shortening

1. Preheat oven to 325°F. Line two large cookie sheets with parchment paper; set aside. In a large food processor combine flour, sugar, oats, butter, baking powder, and salt. Cover and process until mixture resembles fine crumbs.
2. In a large bowl combine eggs, brandy, and vanilla. Stir in flour mixture, almonds, and dried cherries (knead dough with hands if necessary to combine).
3. Divide dough into thirds. Shape each portion into a 9-inch roll. Place rolls 3 inches apart on the prepared cookie sheets. Bake on separate oven racks for 25 to 30 minutes or until a wooden toothpick inserted near the centers comes out clean. Cool on cookie sheets for 45 minutes.
4. Preheat oven to 325°F. Using a serrated knife, cut each roll crosswise into ½-inch slices. Place slices on a large ungreased cookie sheet. Bake for 8 minutes. Carefully turn slices over and bake for 8 to 10 minutes more or until crisp and lightly browned. Transfer to a wire rack; cool.
5. In a medium microwave-safe bowl microwave white chocolate and shortening on 50% power for 1½ to 2 minutes or until melted, stirring two or three times. Drizzle biscotti with melted white chocolate. Let stand until white chocolate is set.
PER SERVING *104 cal., 5 g fat (2 g sat. fat), 14 mg chol., 77 mg sodium, 14 g carb., 1 g fiber, 2 g pro.*

Salted Pumpkin Caramel Thumbprints

PREP **50 minutes** CHILL **5 hours**
BAKE **8 minutes at 375°F**
MAKES **36 servings**

⅔ cup unsalted butter, softened
½ cup packed light brown sugar
¼ teaspoon salt
1 egg
1 teaspoon vanilla
1½ cups all-purpose flour
½ cup granulated sugar
2 tablespoons water
2 tablespoons light-color corn syrup
⅓ cup heavy cream
2 tablespoons unsalted butter
¾ teaspoon pumpkin pie spice
½ cup canned pumpkin
  Coarse sea salt

1. For cookie dough, in a large mixing bowl beat ⅔ cup butter with a mixer on medium to high for 30 seconds. Add brown sugar and ¼ teaspoon salt. Beat until combined, scraping sides of bowl occasionally. Beat in egg and vanilla until combined. Beat in flour. Cover and chill dough about 1 hour or until easy to handle.
2. Preheat oven to 375°F. Roll dough into 1-inch balls. Place 2 inches apart on ungreased cookie sheets. Press thumb into the center of each ball. Bake for 8 to 10 minutes or until bottoms are lightly browned. If cookie centers puff during baking, repress with the back of a measuring spoon. Cool on a wire rack.
3. For Salted Pumpkin Caramel, place granulated sugar, the water, and corn syrup in a medium saucepan. Bring to boiling over medium heat, swirling the pan to stir. Boil gently, uncovered, until browned. Once sugar has browned to medium amber color, for 5 to 8 minutes, remove from heat. Immediately add cream and 2 tablespoons butter (mixture will boil and foam). Stir well. Add pumpkin spice and pumpkin; stir well to incorporate (caramel may seem thin). Place in a bowl. Cover and chill at least 4 hours. Spoon into cooled cookies; sprinkle with sea salt.
PER SERVING *92 cal., 5 g fat (3 g sat. fat), 19 mg chol., 86 mg sodium, 11 g carb., 0 g fiber, 1 g pro.*

PISTACHIO TASSIES

Pistachio Tassies

PREP **25 minutes**
BAKE **18 minutes at 350°F**
COOL **10 minutes**
MAKES **24 servings**

½ cup butter, softened
1 3-ounce package cream cheese, softened
2 tablespoons granulated sugar
1 cup all-purpose flour
½ teaspoon orange zest
1 egg, lightly beaten
1 cup powdered sugar
½ cup finely chopped pistachio nuts
2 tablespoons finely snipped dried apricots

1. Preheat oven to 350°F. For dough, in a medium mixing bowl beat butter, cream cheese, and granulated sugar with a mixer on medium until smooth. Add flour and orange zest, beating on low just until combined.
2. For filling, in a small bowl combine egg, powdered sugar, ⅓ cup of the pistachios, and the dried apricots.
3. Press a scant 1 tablespoon of the dough onto bottoms and up the sides of each of the 24 ungreased 1¾-inch muffin cups. Spoon filling into pastry-lined cups, filling each about three-fourths full. Top with the remaining pistachios.
4. Bake for 18 to 20 minutes or until pastry is golden and filling is puffed and set. Cool in muffin cups on a wire rack for 10 minutes. Remove cookies from muffin cups. Cool completely on wire rack.
PER SERVING *108 cal., 6 g fat (3 g sat. fat), 22 mg chol., 60 mg sodium, 11 g carb., 0 g fiber, 2 g pro.*

CARAMEL APPLE
BARS

Pistachio Bars

PREP 35 minutes CHILL 3 hours
MAKES 25 servings

    1 egg, lightly beaten
  ½ cup butter
  ¼ cup unsweetened cocoa powder
    2 tablespoons granulated sugar
    1 teaspoon vanilla
    2 cups finely crushed cinnamon
       graham crackers
  ½ cup finely chopped pistachio nuts
  ¼ cup butter, softened
  ¼ cup pistachio instant pudding
       and pie filling mix
  ¼ cup half-and-half, light cream,
       or milk
1½ cups powdered sugar
    6 ounces bittersweet chocolate,
       coarsely chopped
  ¼ cup butter
  ½ cup coarsely chopped pistachio
       nuts

1. For crust, line a 9-inch square
baking pan with foil, extending foil
over edges of pan.
2. In a medium saucepan combine
egg, the ½ cup butter, the cocoa
powder, granulated sugar, and vanilla.
Stir over medium-low heat just until
butter is melted and mixture starts
to bubble. Remove from heat. Stir
in crushed graham crackers and the
finely chopped pistachios. Press crust
mixture into baking pan.
3. For filling, in a medium mixing bowl
beat the ¼ cup softened butter, the dry
pudding mix, and half-and-half with
a mixer on medium until combined.
Gradually add powdered sugar, beating
well. Carefully spread filling over crust
in pan. Cover and chill about 1 hour or
until firm.
4. For topping, in a small saucepan stir
chocolate and the ¼ cup butter over
low heat until melted. Spread topping
over filling. Sprinkle with the coarsely
chopped pistachios. Cover and chill for
2 hours or until firm. Using the edges
of the foil, lift uncut bars out of pan.
Cut into bars.
PER SERVING *207 cal., 14 g fat
(7 g sat. fat), 28 mg chol., 154 mg sodium,
21 g carb., 2 g fiber, 3 g pro.*

Caramel Apple Bars

PREP 35 minutes STAND 1 hour
MAKES 16 servings

    1 14-ounce package vanilla
       caramels, unwrapped
    2 tablespoons butter
    3 cups tiny marshmallows
  ¼ teaspoon ground cinnamon
    3 cups crisp rice cereal
    1 cup coarsely snipped dried apples
    2 tablespoons milk
    1 to 2 ounces white baking chocolate
       with cocoa butter, chopped

1. Line an 8-inch square baking pan
with foil, extending the foil over edges
of pan. Butter foil; set pan aside.
2. In a large heavy saucepan heat
and stir half the caramels and the
2 tablespoons butter over medium-
low heat just until melted. Remove

from heat. Stir in marshmallows and
cinnamon until marshmallows are
melted. Add cereal and dried apples,
stirring gently to coat. Transfer to the
pan; press firmly and evenly into pan.
3. In a microwave-safe bowl heat
remaining caramels and the milk for
1½ to 2 minutes or until caramel is
smooth, stirring every 30 seconds.
Spoon caramel over cereal mixture. Let
stand until set. Use foil to lift uncut bars
out of pan. Cut into triangles (hats).
4. In a microwave-safe bowl heat white
baking chocolate for 30 to 60 seconds
or until melted, stirring every
30 seconds. Line a baking sheet with
waxed paper. Dip each hat base into
white chocolate; place on waxed paper.
Insert a lollipop stick into each base.
Let stand until set.
PER SERVING *181 cal., 5 g fat
(4 g sat. fat), 4 mg chol., 112 mg sodium,
32 g carb., 0 g fiber, 2 g pro.*

PISTACHIO
BARS

GRAHAM CRACKER BARS

DANISH PASTRY APPLE BARS

Graham Cracker Bars

PREP **30 minutes** COOL **30 minutes**
CHILL **4 hours** MAKES **24 servings**

¾ cup butter
¾ cup granulated sugar
¼ cup milk
1 egg, lightly beaten
1 cup chopped pecans, toasted
   (tip, page 32)
1 cup graham cracker crumbs
12 graham crackers
1 tablespoon butter, softened
½ cup powdered sugar
2 to 3 teaspoons milk

1. For filling, in a medium saucepan
combine the ¾ cup butter, the
granulated sugar, the ¼ cup milk, and
the egg. Cook and stir over medium
heat until mixture comes to a full
boil. Remove from heat. Stir in pecans
and graham cracker crumbs. Cool for
30 minutes.
2. Line a cookie sheet with foil. Place
six of the graham crackers side by side
on the prepared cookie sheet to make
about a 10×7-inch rectangle. Spoon
filling in small mounds onto rectangle.
Spread filling evenly over crackers,
being careful not to move the crackers.
Top with remaining six graham
crackers. Cover lightly with plastic
wrap and chill at least 4 hours or until
filling is firm. Cut into bars.

3. For icing, in a small bowl beat the
1 tablespoon butter with a whisk
until smooth. Gradually whisk in
powdered sugar and enough of the
2 to 3 teaspoons milk to reach a thick
drizzling consistency. Drizzle bars
with icing. Let stand until icing is set.
PER SERVING *171 cal., 11 g fat
(4 g sat. fat), 26 mg chol., 110 mg sodium,
18 g carb., 1 g fiber, 2 g pro.*

Danish Pastry Apple Bars

PREP **30 minutes**
BAKE **50 minutes at 375°F**
MAKES **32 servings**

2½ cups all-purpose flour
1 teaspoon salt
1 cup shortening
1 egg yolk
   Milk
1 cup cornflakes
8 cups peeled and sliced tart
   cooking apples (8 medium)
¾ to 1 cup granulated sugar
1 teaspoon ground cinnamon
1 egg white, lightly beaten

1. Preheat oven to 375°F. For pastry,
in a large bowl stir together flour and
salt. Using a pastry blender, cut in
shortening until mixture resembles
coarse crumbs. In a glass measuring

cup beat egg yolk lightly with a fork.
Stir in enough milk to measure ⅔ cup
total liquid. Add egg yolk mixture all at
once to flour mixture. Stir lightly with
fork until combined (pastry will be
slightly sticky). Divide pastry in half.
2. On a well-floured surface roll half the
pastry into a 17×12-inch rectangle. Fold
pastry crosswise into thirds. Transfer
to a 15×10×1-inch baking pan and
unfold pastry, pressing to fit into the
bottom and sides of the pan. Sprinkle
with cornflakes; top with apple slices.
In a small bowl stir together granulated
sugar and cinnamon; sprinkle over
apples. Roll the remaining pastry into
a 15×10-inch rectangle. Fold pastry
crosswise into thirds. Place on top of
apples and unfold pastry. Crimp edges
or seal with the tines of a fork. Cut slits
in top pastry; brush surface with beaten
egg white.
3. Bake 50 minutes or until apples
are tender and pastry is light brown,
covering loosely with foil the last
25 minutes. Cool completely in pan on
a wire rack. Cut into bars.
PER SERVING *155 cal., 6 g fat
(2 g sat. fat), 7 mg chol., 83 mg sodium,
23 g carb., 1 g fiber, 2 g pro.*

Peanut Butter Swirl Chocolate Brownies

PREP **25 minutes**
BAKE **20 minutes at 350°F**
MAKES **20 servings**

Nonstick cooking spray
¼ cup butter
¾ cup sugar
⅓ cup water
¾ cup refrigerated or frozen egg product, thawed, or 3 eggs, lightly beaten
¼ cup canola oil
1 teaspoon vanilla
1¼ cups all-purpose flour
1 teaspoon baking powder
¼ cup creamy peanut butter
3 tablespoons milk
½ cup unsweetened cocoa powder
¼ cup miniature semisweet chocolate pieces

1. Preheat oven to 350°F. Line a 9-inch square baking pan with foil, extending the foil over edges of pan. Lightly coat foil with cooking spray.
2. In a medium saucepan heat butter over low heat until melted. Remove from heat. Stir in sugar and the water until sugar is dissolved. Stir in egg, oil, and vanilla. Stir in 1 cup of the flour and the baking powder until combined (batter will be thin).
3. Transfer ½ cup of the batter to a small bowl; whisk in peanut butter and 1 tablespoon of the milk until smooth. In another small bowl stir together the remaining flour and the cocoa powder. Stir cocoa mixture and the remaining 2 tablespoons milk into the original batter; stir in chocolate pieces.
4. Pour the chocolate batter into the prepared baking pan. Spoon the peanut butter batter in small mounds onto chocolate batter. Using a table knife or a narrow metal spatula, swirl batters to marble.
5. Bake for 20 to 25 minutes or until top springs back when lightly touched and a wooden toothpick inserted near the center comes out clean. Cool in pan on a wire rack. Using the edges of the foil, lift uncut brownies out of pan. Cut into bars.

PER SERVING *152 cal., 8 g fat (3 g sat. fat), 6 mg chol., 66 mg sodium, 17 g carb., 0 g fiber, 3 g pro.*

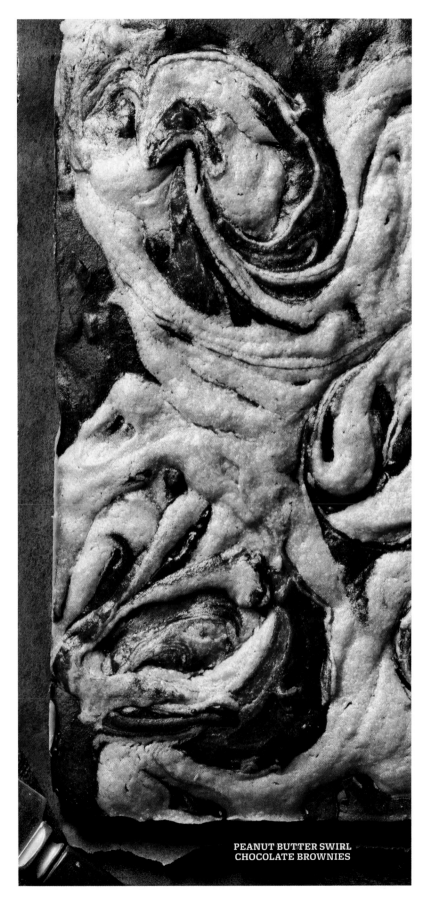

**PEANUT BUTTER SWIRL
CHOCOLATE BROWNIES**

TOFFEE BUTTER
CRUNCH,
PAGE 119

Dreamy Candies

THE OLD-FASHIONED ART of candy-making is
very much in fashion this time of year. Create your
own beautiful confectionary boxes filled with
truffles, nut clusters, toffee, and peanut butter cups.

MARSHMALLOW
TRUFFLES

Marshmallow Truffles

PREP **1 hour** CHILL **1 hour**
FREEZE **20 minutes**
MAKES **48 servings**

- 1 7-ounce jar marshmallow crème
- ⅓ cup butter, softened
- ¼ teaspoon salt
- 1 tablespoon raspberry or orange liqueur
- 3¼ cups powdered sugar
  Powdered sugar
  Whole hazelnuts (filberts), toasted (tip, page 64); pecan halves, whole almonds, whole macadamia nuts, and/or dried cherries
- 8 ounces confetti white candy coating discs
- 1 tablespoon shortening
  Colored candy coating discs, melted (optional)

1. Line a large cookie sheet with waxed paper. Butter waxed paper; set cookie sheet aside. In a large mixing bowl beat marshmallow crème, butter, salt, and liqueur with a mixer on medium until smooth. Gradually add the 3¼ cups powdered sugar, beating well. Cover and chill for 1 hour or until mixture is easy to handle.
2. Using hands lightly dusted with powdered sugar, shape marshmallow mixture into 1-inch balls, forming each ball around a nut half, a whole nut, and/or dried cherry (use more marshmallow mixture to completely cover pecan halves and whole almonds). Place balls on cookie sheet. Cover and freeze for 20 minutes.
3. Meanwhile, in a small heavy saucepan over low heat stir confetti white candy coating discs and shortening until melted and smooth. Remove from heat.
4. Line another large cookie sheet with waxed paper; set aside. Remove balls, a few at a time from freezer. Dip each ball in melted candy coating, letting excess drip back into saucepan. Place truffles on prepared cookie sheet. Chill until coating is set. If desired, drizzle truffles with melted candy coating; let stand until set.
PER SERVING *96 cal., 4 g fat (2 g sat. fat), 3 mg chol., 28 mg sodium, 15 g carb., 1 g fiber, 0 g pro.*

PEANUT BUTTER CUPS

To Store Layer truffles between sheets of waxed paper in an airtight container; cover. Refrigerate up to 1 week or freeze up to 3 months.

Peanut Butter Cups

PREP **30 minutes** CHILL **20 minutes**
MAKES **8 servings**

- 1 cup semisweet chocolate pieces
- ½ cup milk chocolate pieces
- ½ cup chunky peanut butter
- 2 tablespoons chopped peanuts

1. Line eight 2½-inch muffin cups with paper bake cups; set aside.
2. In a small saucepan heat semisweet chocolate pieces and milk chocolate pieces over low heat until melted and smooth. In another small saucepan heat peanut butter over low heat until melted, stirring constantly.
3. Pour about 1 tablespoon melted chocolate into each prepared muffin cup; chill for 5 minutes or until chocolate is firm. Pour about 1 tablespoon melted peanut butter over the chocolate in each cup; chill about 5 minutes or until peanut butter is firm.
4. Pour the remaining melted chocolate over the peanut butter in each cup, spreading to cover peanut butter layer. (If chocolate has stiffened a bit, return pan to low heat and stir chocolate until softened.) Sprinkle top chocolate layer in each cup with peanuts. Chill about 10 minutes or until firm.
PER SERVING *272 cal., 19 g fat (7 g sat. fat), 2 mg chol., 97 mg sodium, 17 g carb., 4 g fiber, 5 g pro.*
To Store Place candy cups in a single layer in an airtight container; cover. Refrigerate up to 2 weeks. Before serving, let stand at room temperature for 5 minutes.

5-Minute Cherry-Walnut Fudge

PREP 5 minutes **CHILL** 30 minutes
MAKES 24 servings

- 1 12-ounce package semisweet chocolate pieces
- ⅔ cup sweetened condensed milk
- ¾ cup snipped dried cherries
- ¾ cup chopped walnuts, toasted if desired (tip, page 32)
- 1 teaspoon vanilla

1. Line a cookie sheet with waxed paper; set aside. In a medium microwave-safe bowl heat chocolate pieces and sweetened condensed milk for 1 minute; stir. Heat for 1 minute or until chocolate is melted and mixture is smooth, stirring every 30 seconds. Stir in ½ cup of the cherries, ¼ cup of the walnuts, and the vanilla.
2. Pour fudge onto the prepared cookie sheet and spread to 9×6 inches. Sprinkle with the remaining ¼ cup cherries and ½ cup walnuts. Chill for 30 minutes or until firm. Cut fudge into 1½-inch squares.
PER SERVING *132 cal., 7 g fat (3 g sat. fat), 3 mg chol., 13 mg sodium, 18 g carb., 1 g fiber, 2 g pro.*
To Store Layer fudge between sheets of waxed paper in an airtight container; cover. Store at room temperature up to 2 days or in the refrigerator up to 1 month.

Orange Cream Fudge

PREP 20 minutes **CHILL** 8 hours
MAKES 72 servings

- 3 cups sugar
- 1 envelope unflavored gelatin
- 1 cup whipping cream
   Pinch salt
- 1 cup unsalted butter
- 12 ounces good quality white baking chocolate, chopped
- 1 7-ounce jar marshmallow creme
- 1 teaspoon orange extract
- ½ teaspoon vanilla bean paste
   Pinch ground nutmeg
   Round red candies (optional)

1. Line a 13×9×2-inch baking pan with parchment paper; set aside.
2. In a large saucepan combine the sugar and gelatin. Stir in cream and salt. Add butter. Stir over medium heat until the butter is melted and sugar is dissolved (the mixture will just begin to simmer). Remove from heat. Add the chocolate, marshmallow creme, orange extract, vanilla bean paste, and nutmeg. Stir until no fluffs of creme remain. Pour into prepared pan.
3. Cover loosely and chill 8 hours or overnight. When fudge is firm, use parchment to lift it out of pan. Cut into diamond-shape pieces. Top each with a red candy, if desired.
PER SERVING *102 cal., 5 g fat (3 g sat. fat), 12 mg chol., 9 mg sodium, 14 g carb., 0 g fiber, 0 g pro.*

Macadamia Clusters

PREP 25 minutes **CHILL** 1 hour
MAKES 24 servings

- 1 cup milk chocolate pieces
- 6 ounces chocolate-flavor candy coating, chopped
- 1 cup chopped dry-roasted macadamia nuts
- ¾ cup snipped dried apricots
   Finely chopped macadamia nuts and/or snipped dried apricots (optional)

1. Line twenty-four 1¾-inch muffin cups with paper bake cups or line a cookie sheet with waxed paper; set aside.
2. In a medium saucepan heat chocolate pieces and candy coating over low heat until melted. Remove from heat; cool slightly. Stir in the 1 cup macadamia nuts and the ¾ cup dried apricots.
3. Drop candy by rounded teaspoons into the prepared muffin cups or onto cookie sheet. If desired, sprinkle with additional macadamia nuts and/or dried apricots. Chill for 1 hour or until firm. Store, covered, in the refrigerator.
PER SERVING *137 cal., 10 g fat (5 g sat. fat), 3 mg chol., 27 mg sodium, 14 g carb., 1 g fiber, 1 g pro.*

ORANGE CREAM FUDGE

MACADAMIA
CLUSTERS

Macadamia
CLUSTERS

DULCE DE LECHE
PRETZEL BITES

Dulce de Leche Pretzel Bites

START TO FINISH 1 hour
MAKES 50 servings

- ¼ cup butter, softened
- ½ cup packed brown sugar
- ¼ cup granulated sugar
- ¼ cup dulce de leche
- 1 tablespoon milk
- 1¼ cups all-purpose flour
- 100 chocolate-covered small pretzel twists
- 24 ounces vanilla-flavor candy coating, chopped
  Assorted red, green, and/or white sprinkles

1. Line a large cookie sheet with waxed paper; set aside. In a medium mixing bowl beat butter with a mixer on medium to high for 30 seconds. Add brown sugar, granulated sugar, dulce de leche, and milk. Beat until combined, scraping sides of bowl occasionally. Beat in flour on low until combined.
2. Shape dough into fifty ½-inch balls. Place each ball on a pretzel. Top with the remaining pretzels; gently press top pretzels down.
3. In a medium saucepan heat candy coating over low heat until melted. Remove from heat; cool for 15 minutes. Using a long-tined fork, hold each pretzel bite over saucepan and spoon over melted coating to cover, letting excess drip back into pan. Place coated pretzel bites on cookie sheet. Sprinkle with assorted sprinkles. Let stand until coating is set.
PER SERVING 179 cal., 9 g fat (6 g sat. fat), 4 mg chol., 105 mg sodium, 24 g carb., 0 g fiber, 1 g pro.

Chocolate-Peanut-Marshmallow Clusters

PREP 20 minutes CHILL 1 hour
MAKES 45 servings

- 6 ounces chocolate-flavor candy coating, coarsely chopped
- 1 cup semisweet chocolate pieces
- 1 cup creamy peanut butter
- 1 10-ounce package tiny marshmallows

- 1½ cups honey-roasted or dry-roasted peanuts

1. Line two cookie sheets with waxed paper; set aside. In a medium-size heavy saucepan stir candy coating, chocolate pieces, and peanut butter over medium-low heat until mixture is melted and smooth. Remove from heat.
2. In a large bowl combine marshmallows and peanuts. Pour chocolate mixture over marshmallow mixture, stirring to coat. Drop candy by heaping tablespoons onto cookie sheets. If desired, sprinkle with additional chopped honey-roasted peanuts. Chill for 1 hour or until set.
PER SERVING 108 cal., 7 g fat (2 g sat. fat), 0 mg chol., 51 mg sodium, 11 g carb., 1 g fiber, 2 g pro.

Toffee Butter Crunch

(photo page 112)

PREP 25 minutes COOK 12 minutes
COOL 4 minutes STAND 3 hours
MAKES 24 servings

- 1 cup butter
- 1 cup sugar
- 3 tablespoons water
- 1 tablespoon light-color corn syrup
- ¾ cup milk chocolate pieces or semisweet chocolate pieces
- ½ to ¾ cup chopped glazed nuts, or regular nuts, toasted (tip, page 32)

1. Line a 13×9×2-inch baking pan with foil, extending foil over edges of pan; set pan aside.
2. In a 2-quart heavy saucepan melt butter over low heat. Stir in sugar, the water, and corn syrup. Bring to boiling over medium-high heat, stirring until sugar is dissolved. Avoid splashing side of saucepan. Clip a candy thermometer to side of pan. Cook over medium heat, stirring frequently, until thermometer registers 290°F, soft-crack stage (about 12 minutes). Mixture should boil at a moderate, steady rate with bubbles over entire surface. Adjust heat as necessary to maintain a steady boil and watch temperature carefully during the last 5 minutes of cooking

because temperature can increase quickly at the end. Remove from heat; remove thermometer.
3. Carefully pour corn syrup mixture into prepared pan; spread evenly. Cool 4 to 5 minutes or just until top is set. Sprinkle evenly with chocolate pieces; let stand for 2 minutes. Spread softened chocolate into an even layer over toffee layer. Sprinkle with nuts; lightly press into chocolate. Let stand at room temperature about 3 hours or until chocolate is set. Use foil to lift candy out of pan; break into pieces.
4. Store with waxed paper between the layers in an airtight container at room temperature for up to 2 weeks.
PER SERVING 141 cal., 10 g fat (6 g sat. fat), 22 mg chol., 59 mg sodium, 12 g carb., 0 g fiber, 1 g pro.

CHOCOLATE-PEANUT-MARSHMALLOW CLUSTERS

EASY CARAMEL-CRACKER CANDY

melted and mixture is smooth, stirring every 30 seconds. For chocolate, in a bowl combine the chocolate pieces and shortening. Heat as directed above.

Malted-Milk Crispy Treats

START TO FINISH 25 minutes
MAKES 24 servings

- ¼ cup butter
- 1 10-ounce package tiny marshmallows
- 1 13-ounce jar marshmallow crème
- ½ cup malted milk powder
- 2 teaspoons vanilla
- 7 cups crisp rice cereal
- ¾ cup coarsely chopped malted milk balls
  Hot-fudge-flavor ice cream topping, warmed (optional)

1. Line a 9×9×2-inch baking pan with foil, extending foil over edges of pan. Generously butter foil.
2. In a 4-quart heavy Dutch oven heat the ¼ cup butter over low heat until melted. Stir in marshmallows. Stir until marshmallows are melted. Stir in marshmallow crème, malted milk powder, and vanilla until combined. Remove ½ cup of the marshmallow mixture; set aside. Add cereal to the remaining marshmallow mixture, stirring gently to coat.
3. Transfer cereal mixture to the prepared baking pan. Using a buttered spatula or buttered piece of waxed paper, press mixture firmly and evenly into pan. Spread the reserved marshmallow mixture over cereal mixture. Sprinkle with malted milk balls; press down gently.
4. Using edges of the foil, lift uncut bars out of pan. Using a long buttered knife, cut into bars. If desired, drizzle with hot fudge topping before serving.
PER SERVING *183 cal., 3 g fat (2 g sat. fat), 7 mg chol., 117 mg sodium, 36 g carb., 0 g fiber, 2 g pro.*

Easy Caramel-Cracker Candy

START TO FINISH 15 minutes
MAKES 36 servings

- 12 to 15 chocolate or plain graham crackers
- 1 14-ounce package vanilla caramels, unwrapped
- ¼ cup half-and-half or light cream
- 1½ cups semisweet chocolate pieces
- 1 tablespoon shortening
- 1 cup chopped toasted hazelnuts (filberts) (tip, page 64) or almonds (tip, page 32)

1. Line a 15×10×1-inch baking pan with foil, extending foil over edges of pan. Grease foil. In the prepared pan arrange enough of the graham crackers side by side to completely cover pan bottom, breaking to fit as necessary.

2. In a medium heavy saucepan cook and stir caramels and half-and-half over medium-low heat until mixture is smooth.* Pour caramel mixture over graham crackers in pan.
3. In a small heavy saucepan cook and stir chocolate and shortening over medium-low heat until melted and smooth.* Pour melted chocolate mixture over caramel in pan, spreading evenly. Sprinkle with nuts. Let stand until set. Using the edges of the foil, lift uncut candy out of pan. Cut into squares.
PER SERVING *149 cal., 7 g fat (3 g sat. fat), 1 mg chol., 92 mg sodium, 21 g carb., 1 g fiber, 2 g pro.*
*Tip If you prefer, use a microwave to melt the caramels and chocolate. For caramels, in a medium-size microwave-safe bowl combine caramels and half-and-half. Heat for 1½ to 2 minutes or until caramels are

EGGS AND BACON BREAKFAST
CASSEROLE, PAGE 125

CANDIED CANDY
CANES, PAGE 133

Tasteful Gifts

SHARE YOUR APPRECIATION of friends, teachers, and holiday-party hosts with a gift from your kitchen—so much more meaningful than something from the mall. This selection of yummy casseroles, breads, jams, and sweet treats makes "shopping" a pleasure.

Paprika Sesame Breadsticks

PREP 20 minutes
BAKE 15 minutes per batch at 400°F
MAKES 18 servings

1 egg, lightly beaten
1 tablespoon water
1 teaspoon toasted sesame oil
1 17.3-ounce package frozen puff pastry sheets (2 sheets), thawed
½ teaspoon smoked paprika or ¼ teaspoon ground chipotle chile pepper
¼ teaspoon sea salt
2 tablespoons white and/or black sesame seeds

1. Preheat oven to 400°F. Line two large baking sheets with parchment paper or foil. Grease foil, if using. In a bowl combine egg, the water, and sesame oil. Unfold one pastry sheet. Brush with some of the egg mixture. In another bowl combine paprika and salt. Sprinkle half the paprika mixture on the pastry. Fold pastry in half to form a rectangle, aligning edges and pressing to seal. Brush top of pastry with more egg mixture. Sprinkle top with half the sesame seeds.

2. With a sharp knife cut pastry lengthwise into ½-inch strips. Twist each strip five or six times and place 1 inch apart on one of the prepared baking sheets, pressing ends down.

3. Bake for 15 minutes or until golden. Repeat with remaining pastry sheet, egg mixture, paprika mixture, and sesame seeds.

PER SERVING 162 cal., 11 g fat (3 g sat. fat), 12 mg chol., 94 mg sodium, 13 g carb., 1 g fiber, 3 g pro.

To give as a gift Fold scrapbooking paper to 7×5 inches. Using a glue stick, closed the open long side and one narrow side to make a long pocket. Cut another piece of scrapbooking paper into a 5-inch circle with scallop-edge scissors. Using straight scissors, cut circle in half. Glue each semicircle to the front on each narrow end of pocket. Attach a brad near the round edge of each semicircle. Run ribbon between brads, attaching by twisting ends around brads.

Whole Wheat Sweet Potato Bread

PREP 30 minutes
BAKE 30 minutes at 375°F
COOL 10 minutes
MAKES 16 servings

Nonstick cooking spray
¾ cup all-purpose flour
¾ cup white whole wheat flour or whole wheat flour
2 teaspoons baking powder
1 teaspoon pumpkin pie spice
½ teaspoon baking soda
¼ teaspoon salt
½ cup light sour cream
½ cup refrigerated or 2 eggs, lightly beaten
¼ cup sugar
¼ cup fat-free milk
¼ cup canola oil
1½ teaspoons vanilla
1 cup mashed cooked peeled sweet potatoes
¼ cup chopped pitted dates
¼ cup chopped pecans, toasted (tip, page 32)

1. Preheat oven to 375°F. Lightly coat three 5¾×3×2-inch pans with cooking spray. Set aside.

2. In a bowl combine flours, baking powder, pumpkin pie spice, baking soda, and salt. In another bowl combine sour cream, egg product, sugar, milk, oil, and vanilla. Stir in sweet potatoes. Add sour cream mixture all at once to flour mixture. Stir just until moistened. Fold in dates and nuts. Evenly spoon batter into pans.

3. Bake for 30 to 40 minutes or until a toothpick inserted near centers comes out clean. Cool in pans on a wire rack for 10 minutes. Remove from pans. Cool completely.

PER SERVING 132 cal., 5 g fat (1 g sat. fat), 2 mg chol., 132 mg sodium, 19 g carb., 2 g fiber, 3 g pro.

To give as a gift Wrap loaves in plastic wrap and place in the center of a paper coffee filter. Cut a circle from a sheet of scrapbooking paper and center it on the bread loaf. Tie it all together with sheer ribbon.

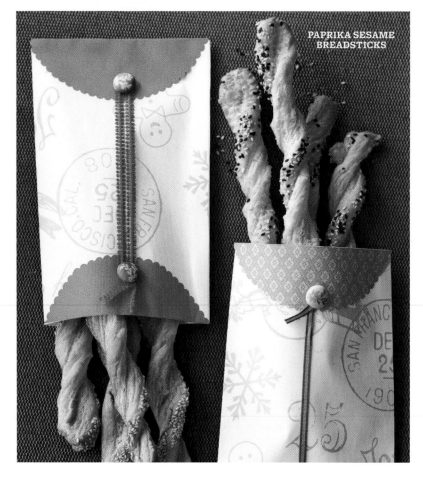

PAPRIKA SESAME BREADSTICKS

WHOLE WHEAT
SWEET POTATO
BREAD

REINDEER
COOKIES

Reindeer Cookies

PREP 40 minutes
BAKE 8 minutes at 350°F
MAKES 64 servings

½ cup butter, softened
½ cup shortening
1 cup sugar
¼ cup unsweetened cocoa powder
1 teaspoon baking powder
¼ teaspoon salt
1 egg
1 teaspoon vanilla
2¼ cups all-purpose flour
  Canned chocolate frosting
  Miniature pretzel twists
  Miniature candy-coated milk
  chocolate pieces
  Red candy-coated chocolate-
  covered peanuts

1. In a mixing bowl beat butter and shortening with a mixer on medium to high for 30 seconds. Add sugar, cocoa powder, baking powder, and salt. Beat until combined, scraping bowl occasionally. Beat in egg and vanilla until combined. Beat in as much of the flour as you can. Stir in any remaining flour. Divide dough in half. If necessary, cover and chill dough about 1 hour or until easy to handle.
2. Preheat oven to 350°F. On a lightly floured surface roll half the dough at a time to ¼-inch thickness. Cut with a 2-inch triangle cookie cutter. (Or shape each half of dough into an 8-inch square. Cut each square into sixteen 2-inch squares. Cut each 2-inch square in half diagonally to make 64 triangles total.) Place triangles 2 inches apart on an ungreased baking sheet.
3. Bake for 8 to 10 minutes or until edges are light brown. Transfer to wire racks to cool.
4. For each reindeer, pipe a little frosting on two pretzels; attach to one side of each cookie for antlers. Use frosting to attach a chocolate-covered peanut for a nose. Pipe a little frosting on milk chocolate pieces and attach for eyes. Let stand until frosting is set.
PER SERVING *78 cal., 4 g fat (2 g sat. fat), 7 mg chol., 55 mg sodium, 10 g carb., 0 g fiber, 1 g pro.*
To give as a gift Layer cookies between waxed paper in a rectangular plastic storage container; cover. Cut a

EASY STRAWBERRY JAM

piece of brown felt into a triangle the width of the lid; attach to the lid using fabric glue. Add two craft eyes and a black pom-pom for the nose using fabric glue. For antlers, twist a 3-inch piece of pipe cleaner around each end of one long pipe cleaner. Twist the long pipe cleaner around a headband then place the headband on the width of the container.

Easy Strawberry Jam

PREP 30 minutes
STAND 10 minutes + 24 hours
MAKES 6 servings

4 cups fresh strawberries, hulled
4 cups sugar
1 1¾-ounce package unflavored powdered fruit pectin
¾ cup water
2 tablespoons fresh lemon juice
1 small lemon, very thinly sliced

1. In large bowl crush berries with masher. Stir in sugar. Let stand 10 minutes; stirring occasionally.

2. In a small saucepan combine pectin and the water. Bring to boiling; boil 1 minute, stirring constantly. Remove from heat. Pour into berry mixture. Add lemon juice and stir 3 minutes or until sugar is dissolved and mixture is smooth. Stir in lemon slices.
3. Ladle jam into clean half-pint jars or freezer containers, leaving ½-inch headspace. Seal and label. Let stand at room temperature 24 hours or until set*. Refrigerate up to 3 weeks; or freeze up to 1 year then thaw in refrigerator to use. Makes 2½ cups.
PER SERVING *87 cal., 0 g fat, 0 mg chol., 3 mg sodium, 23 g carb., 0 g fiber, 0 g pro.*
***Tip** Do not double recipe. Freezer jam does not set as firmly as cooked jam.
To give as a gift Cut a sleeve from an old sweater 1 inch longer than the height of a 2-cup plastic container. Slide the sleeve over the container. Tie a small jam spoon to the front of the container with a ribbon. Attach a paper snowflake to the lid using crafts glue.

Sandies

PREP 35 minutes CHILL 2½ hours
BAKE 12 minutes at 325°F
MAKES 30 servings

- 1 cup butter, softened
- ½ cup powdered sugar
- 1 tablespoon water
- 1 teaspoon vanilla
- 2 cups all-purpose flour
- 1½ cups finely chopped pecans, toasted
- 1 cup powdered sugar

1. In a large mixing bowl beat butter with a mixer on medium to high for 30 seconds. Add the ½ cup powdered sugar. Beat until combined, scraping sides of bowl occasionally. Beat in the water and vanilla until combined. Beat in as much of the flour as you can. Stir in remaining flour and the pecans. Wrap dough and chill 30 to 60 minutes or until firm enough to shape.
2. Preheat oven to 325°F. Divide dough into two portions. Shape each dough portion into a 5½×2½-inch-diameter log. Wrap logs in plastic wrap and chill for 2 hours or until firm. Cut logs into ¼-inch slices. Place 1 inch apart on ungreased cookie sheets. Bake for 12 to 15 minutes or until bottoms are light brown. Cool on wire racks. Place the 1 cup powdered sugar in a large shallow bowl. Add cooled cookies, in batches, to bowl. Turn to coat.
PER SERVING *134 cal., 10 g fat (4 g sat. fat), 16 mg chol., 54 mg sodium, 10 g carb., 1 g fiber, 1 g pro.*

To give as a gift Using heavy copy paper, make a photocopy of a vintage towel. Position the paper copy, printed side up, on scrapbooking paper printed side down. Using scallop-edge scissors, cut a stocking shape approximately 9 inches long and 5 inches wide. From scrapbooking paper, cut two 3×5-inch strips for the top bands and two half circles for the toe pieces. Using crafts glue, run a bead along both sides of stocking, leaving an opening at the top. Attach the top bands and the toe pieces on the front and back using a glue stick. Add ribbon to the band and toe. Let glue dry completely before filling with cookies.

SANDIES

Christmas Macaroon Mix

START TO FINISH 15 minutes
MAKES 12 servings

- 1 7-ounce package flaked coconut (2⅔ cups)
- ⅔ cup sugar
- ½ cup chopped almonds, toasted
- ¼ cup all-purpose flour
- ¼ teaspoon salt
- ¼ cup chopped candied red and/or green cherries
- 2 tablespoons finely chopped candied orange peel

1. In a wide-mouth 1-quart jar layer each ingredient in the order listed*. Fasten lid; attach directions for making macaroons to jar. Makes 1 jar (enough for 30 cookies).
2. To make 30 macaroons, preheat oven to 325°F. Line cookie sheets with parchment paper or foil. Grease foil, if using. In a medium bowl stir together the contents of the jar. Add 3 lightly beaten egg whites, stirring well to combine. Drop dough by teaspoons 2 inches apart on prepared cookie sheets. Bake for 15 to 18 minutes or until light brown. Cool cookies on a wire rack.
PER SERVING *83 cal., 5 g fat (4 g sat. fat), 0 mg chol., 57 mg sodium, 9 g carb., 1 g fiber, 2 g pro.*

To give a gift Trace the disk lid on scrapbooking paper and cut out. Fill the jar with the cookie mix. Place the disk lid on the jar, then place the scrapbooking paper circle on top. Secure the rim lid around the paper and disk. Twist a white pipe cleaner onto each end of one red pipe cleaner. Position the center of the red pipe cleaner underneath the jar and bring the white pipe cleaners up the sides of the jar, twisting the ends together at the top. Affix a scrapbooking sticker to the front of the jar and label the jar. Include baking directions with the gift.
*Tip Use a wide-mouth funnel when adding layers of ingredients to the jar.

Christmas
Macaroon
•Mix•

BEST-EVER NUT
BRITTLE

Best-Ever Nut Brittle

PREP **10 minutes** COOL **1 hour**
MICROWAVE **8 minutes**
MAKES **36 servings**

1 cup sugar
½ cup light-color corn syrup
⅛ teaspoon salt
⅛ teaspoon ground cardamom
½ cup whole cashews
½ cup pistachios
½ cup pecan halves
1 tablespoon butter
1 teaspoon baking soda
1 teaspoon vanilla

1. Grease a large baking sheet; set aside. In a 2-quart microwave-safe bowl combine sugar, corn syrup, salt, and cardamom. Microwave, uncovered, on high for 6 minutes, stirring once halfway through cooking time.
2. Stir in cashews, pistachios, pecans, and butter. Microwave, uncovered, on high for 2 minutes or just until mixture turns golden (mixture continues to cook and becomes more golden when removed from the microwave).
3. Quickly stir in baking soda and vanilla. Spread thinly and evenly on the prepared baking sheet. Let cool. Break into pieces.
PER SERVING *70 cal., 3 g fat (1 g sat. fat), 1 mg chol., 69 mg sodium, 10 g carb., 0 g fiber, 1 g pro.*
To give as a gift Thread five or six small bells onto a 12-inch length of jewelry crafting wire. Twist each end of the wire around bucket handle. Using clear tape, tape one end of silver garland to the bottom of the bucket then wrap the garland around the bucket to cover. Tape the opposite end of the garland to the bucket. Hang mini ball ornaments from the garland and bucket rim.

Candied Candy Canes

PREP **25 minutes** STAND **1 hour**
MAKES **12 servings**

1 cup white baking pieces or semisweet chocolate pieces
1 teaspoon shortening
12 candy canes, about 5½ inches long
Decorative red sugar, nonpareils, and/or jimmies

1. In a small saucepan combine baking pieces and shortening. Stir over low heat until melted. (Or combine baking pieces and shortening in a microwave-safe bowl. Heat on 70% power for 1 to 2 minutes or until baking pieces are melted, stirring every 30 seconds.)

2. Transfer melted baking pieces to a 1-cup glass liquid measure. Dip the top half of each candy cane into the melted chocolate, tilting cup if necessary to coat candy cane. Immediately sprinkle with or roll in decorative sugar, nonpareils, or jimmies. Place on a waxed paper-lined baking sheet. Let stand at least 1 hour or until chocolate is firm.
PER SERVING *227 cal., 6 g fat (5 g sat. fat), 0 mg chol., 37 mg sodium, 41 g carb., 0 g fiber, 0 g pro.*
To give as a gift Lay a string of crafting beads on a flat surface and, using a wooden crafts stick, rub on press-on letter decals. Tie the string of beads around a glass vase. Fill the bottom third of the base with granulated or coarse sugar. Stand the candy canes handles in the sugar.

CANDIED CANDY CANES

CHEESE FONDUE,
PAGE 136

Raise Your Glass

RING IN THE NEW YEAR in style with a spread of sophisticated and celebratory fare. From elegant appetizers to black-tie desserts, this selection of party-perfect recipes will help you welcome the coming year in great taste.

Stuffed Endive with Pear, Walnut, and Goat Cheese

START TO FINISH 25 minutes
MAKES 6 servings

- 1 tablespoon olive oil
- 2 teaspoons lemon juice
  Salt and black pepper
- 1 firm medium pear, such as Bartlett, cored and thinly sliced lengthwise
- ¼ cup coarsely chopped walnuts (toasted, if desired)
- ¼ cup loosely packed fresh Italian parsley leaves
- 4 ounces goat cheese, crumbled
- 12 endive leaves (1 large head)
  Honey (optional)

1. In a medium bowl whisk together olive oil and lemon juice. Season with salt and pepper. Add pear, walnuts, parsley, and goat cheese. Toss to coat.
2. Spoon pear filling into endive leaves. Arrange stuffed endive on a serving platter. If desired, drizzle with honey.
PER SERVING 140 cal., 11 g fat (5 g sat. fat), 15 mg chol., 197 mg sodium, 6 g carb., 1 g fiber, 5 g pro.

Cheese Fondue

(photo on page 134)

PREP 30 minutes
SLOW COOK 4 hours (low)
MAKES 36 servings

- 3 cups reduced-sodium chicken broth
- 3 cups whipping cream
- 1 cup dry white wine
- 3 cloves garlic, minced
- ½ cup butter, softened
- ½ cup all-purpose flour
- 1 teaspoon lemon zest
- 16 ounces shredded Havarti cheese
- 2 5.2-ounce containers semisoft cheese with garlic and fine herbes
  Cracked black pepper
  French bread cubes; steamed broccoli; boiled potatoes; cherry tomatoes; orange, yellow, and/or red bell peppers

1. In a 4- to 5-quart slow cooker combine broth, whipping cream, wine, and garlic. Cover and cook on low-heat setting for 4 to 5 hours.
2. In a medium bowl stir together butter and flour until a paste forms. Stir into hot broth mixture until combined. Cover and cook about 30 minutes more or until slightly thickened.
3. Whisk lemon zest into broth mixture. Gradually whisk in Havarti cheese and semisoft cheese until smooth. Sprinkle with cracked black pepper. Serve with bread cubes, broccoli, potatoes, cherry tomatoes, and/or bell peppers.
PER SERVING 173 cal., 17 g fat (11 g sat. fat), 43 mg chol., 186 mg sodium, 2 g carb., 0 g fiber, 4 g pro.

Cheddar-Beer Fondue Prepare using the same method, substituting the following ingredients: lager beer for the wine, 1 tablespoon spicy brown mustard for the lemon zest, use cheddar cheese for the Havarti, and shredded sharp cheddar for the semisoft cheese.

Mexican Eggnog

PREP 25 minutes
CHILL 4 hours
MAKES 10 servings

- 8 egg yolks, lightly beaten
- 4 cups whole milk
- ⅔ cup sugar
- 1 cinnamon stick
- 1 vanilla bean or 1 teaspoon vanilla
- ⅓ to ½ cup light-color rum
  Ground nutmeg (optional)

1. In a large heavy saucepan combine egg yolks, milk, sugar, cinnamon stick, and the vanilla bean (if using). Cook and stir over medium heat about 10 minutes or just until eggnog coats a metal spoon. Remove from heat. Place the saucepan in a sink or bowl of ice water and stir eggnog for 2 minutes. Remove cinnamon stick and vanilla bean. Using a sharp knife, halve vanilla bean lengthwise and use the tip of the knife to scrape out the seeds. Add seeds to eggnog; discard bean. Transfer to a pitcher.
2. Stir in rum and vanilla (if using). Cover and chill for 4 to 24 hours before serving. If desired, sprinkle the pitcher or each serving with ground nutmeg.
PER SERVING 173 cal., 7 g fat (3 g sat. fat), 178 mg chol., 46 mg sodium, 19 g carb., 0 g fiber, 5 g pro.

STUFFED ENDIVE WITH PEAR, WALNUT, AND GOAT CHEESE

MEXICAN
EGGNOG

Rosemary-Roasted Loin of Pork

PREP 30 minutes
ROAST 1 hour at 375°F
STAND 15 minutes MAKES 8 servings

1 cup sliced leeks (3 medium)
2 tablespoons snipped fresh basil
3 to 4 teaspoons snipped fresh rosemary
2 cloves garlic, minced
½ teaspoon salt
¼ teaspoon freshly ground black pepper
2 tablespoons olive oil
1 2½-pound boneless pork top loin roast (single loin)
2 sprigs fresh rosemary

1. Preheat oven to 375°F. In a food processor combine leeks, basil, snipped rosemary, garlic, salt, and pepper. Add 1 tablespoon of the oil. Cover and process until mixture forms a chunky paste.
2. Trim fat from meat. Cut meat in half lengthwise. Spread half the leek mixture on cut sides of meat. Place cut sides together and tie tightly with 100%-cotton kitchen string. Thread rosemary sprigs through string on meat. Using a skewer, poke holes in the top and sides of meat; brush with the remaining 1 tablespoon oil. Spread the remaining leek mixture over meat. Place meat on a rack in a shallow roasting pan.
3. Roast, uncovered, for 1 to 1½ hours or until juices run clear (150°F). Transfer meat to a serving platter. Cover with foil; let stand for 15 minutes before carving. (Temperature of meat after standing should be 160°F.)

PER SERVING *239 cal., 11 g fat (3 g sat. fat), 83 mg chol., 206 mg sodium, 2 g carb., 0 g fiber, 31 g pro.*

Tip: It is essential to let cooked meat or poultry rest for 10 to 15 minutes before serving. This allows the flavorful juices to absorb back into the meat rather than spilling out when cut.
Make Ahead Prepare as directed through Step 2. Cover and chill for up to 24 hours. To serve, let stand at room temperature for 30 minutes. Roast as directed.

Caramelized Shallot BLT Soup

START TO FINISH 40 minutes
MAKES 4 main-dish or 6 side-dish servings

4 slices bacon
1½ cups sliced shallots (12 medium)
3 14.5-ounce cans reduced-sodium chicken broth
1 cup seeded and chopped roma tomatoes (3 medium)
2¼ cups coarsely chopped escarole or arugula

1. In a large skillet cook bacon over medium heat until crisp. Drain bacon on paper towels, reserving 1 tablespoon drippings in skillet. Coarsely crumble bacon; set aside.
2. Add shallots to the reserved drippings. Cook, covered, over medium-low heat for 13 to 15 minutes or until tender, stirring occasionally. Continue cooking, uncovered, over medium-high heat for 3 to 5 minutes or until golden, stirring frequently.
3. Transfer shallots to a large saucepan; add broth and tomatoes. Bring to boiling; reduce heat. Simmer for 5 minutes. Stir in escarole; cook for 5 minutes more. Top each serving with crumbled bacon.

PER MAIN-DISH SERVING *154 cal., 6 g fat (2 g sat. fat), 11 mg chol., 871 mg sodium, 16 g carb., 4 g fiber, 10 g pro.*

Maple-Brined Chicken with Roasted Vegetables

PREP 1 hour CHILL 12 hours
ROAST 1 hour 45 minutes at 400°F
STAND 15 minutes
MAKES 6 servings

1 cup kosher salt
½ cup packed brown sugar
4 cups apple juice or apple cider
4 cups water
1 cup pure maple syrup
2 tablespoons stone-ground Dijon mustard
1 5- to 6-pound roasting chicken
6 large carrots, cut into 2-inch chunks

CARAMELIZED SHALLOT BLT SOUP

MAPLE-BRINED CHICKEN WITH ROASTED VEGETABLES

2 large onions, cut into ½-inch slices

2 fennel bulbs, trimmed and cut into wedges

4 cloves garlic, peeled and halved

6 sprigs fresh thyme

3 tablespoons olive oil
Salt and black pepper

1 medium orange, halved

1. For brine, in an extra-large stainless-steel stockpot combine the kosher salt and brown sugar; stir in apple juice, the water, maple syrup, and mustard. Cook and stir over medium-high heat until salt and sugar are completely dissolved. Remove from heat and cool to room temperature.

2. Remove giblets from chicken, if present (reserve for another use if desired). Rinse chicken inside and out with cool water. Place chicken in stockpot, thoroughly immersed in brine. Cover stockpot. Chill for 12 hours.

3. In a resealable plastic bag combine carrots, onions, fennel, garlic, and two sprigs of the thyme; drizzle olive oil over vegetables. Seal bag; massage vegetables to evenly coat with oil. Chill up to 12 hours.

4. Preheat oven to 400°F. Remove chicken from brine; discard brine. Pat chicken dry both inside and out with paper towels. Sprinkle chicken cavity with salt and pepper. Place orange halves and the remaining four sprigs thyme in cavity. Skewer neck skin to back. Tie legs to tail. Twist wing tips under back. Spread vegetables evenly in a roasting pan. Place chicken, breast side up, on vegetables.

5. Roast for 1¾ to 2¼ hours or until a thermometer inserted into center of an inside thigh muscle registers 180°F. Remove chicken and vegetables from oven. Tent loosely with foil; let stand for 15 minutes before carving. Serve with roasted vegetables.

PER SERVING 692 cal., 44 g fat (12 g sat. fat), 191 mg chol., 405 mg sodium, 22 g carb., 6 g fiber, 50 g pro.

TART CHERRY
CRANBERRY RELISH

Tart Cherry Cranberry Relish

PREP 30 minutes COOL 2 hours
CHILL 3 hours MAKES 20 servings

- 4 oranges
- ⅔ cup packed dark brown sugar
- ½ cup dry white wine
- 2 4-inch sprigs fresh rosemary
- 1 3-inch cinnamon stick
- ¼ teaspoon freshly ground black pepper
- 2 12-ounce bags fresh cranberries
- 1½ cups dried tart cherries

1. Remove zest from one orange; wrap in plastic wrap and chill until needed. Juice oranges to equal 1 cup. In a large saucepan bring orange juice, brown sugar, wine, rosemary, cinnamon stick, and pepper to boiling, stirring until sugar is dissolved. Discard rosemary.
2. Add cranberries and cherries. Cook over medium heat for 8 minutes or until cherries are plump and cranberries burst. Reduce heat and simmer, uncovered, for 5 minutes on low. Cool for 2 hours. Remove and discard cinnamon stick. Cover and chill for 3 hours.
3. Sprinkle with reserved orange zest before serving.

PER SERVING *83 cal., 0 g fat, 0 mg chol., 5 mg sodium, 22 g carb., 2 g fiber, 1 g pro.*

Beer-Steamed Mussels with Sausage and Fennel

START TO FINISH 35 minutes
MAKES 6 servings

- 2 teaspoons olive oil
- 4 ounces uncooked hot Italian turkey sausage link, casing removed
- 6 cloves garlic, thinly sliced
- 1 cup onion, chopped
- ½ cup thinly sliced fennel
- 1 teaspoon fennel seeds
- ½ teaspoon salt
- ½ teaspoon crushed red pepper
- 1 cup seeded and chopped tomatoes
- 1 12-ounce bottle mild beer
- 1 cup reduced-sodium chicken broth

BEER-STEAMED MUSSELS WITH SAUSAGE AND FENNEL

- 2 pounds fresh black mussels, scrubbed, rinsed, and beards removed
- 1 lemon, cut into 6 wedges
- ⅓ cup snipped fresh Italian parsley
  Sliced crusty bread (optional)
  Lemon wedges (optional)

1. In an extra-large skillet with a tight-fitting lid heat oil over medium heat. Add sausage; cook until browned, using a spoon to break up meat as it cooks. Using a slotted spoon, drain sausage on paper towels, reserving drippings in skillet.
2. Add garlic to the reserved drippings; cook and stir about 2 minutes or just until golden. Stir in onion, sliced fennel, fennel seeds, salt, and crushed red pepper. Cook, covered, about 5 minutes or until vegetables are tender. Stir in tomatoes and cooked sausage.
3. Increase heat to high. Add beer and broth to skillet; bring to boiling. Stir in mussels and lemon wedges. Cook, covered, for 2 to 3 minutes or just until mussels open. Discard any mussels that do not open. Sprinkle with parsley. Serve mussels in bowls with broth mixture and, if desired, crusty bread and additional lemon wedges.

PER SERVING *230 cal., 7 g fat (1 g sat. fat), 55 mg chol., 854 mg sodium, 15 g carb., 2 g fiber, 23 g pro.*

CREAM CHEESE
MASHERS WITH
KALE PESTO

Cream Cheese Mashers with Kale Pesto

PREP 30 minutes COOK 20 minutes
MAKES 22 servings

- 6 cups chopped kale leaves and stems (¾ large bunch; 6 ounces)
- ¾ cup olive oil
- 6 cloves garlic, peeled
- ¾ cup grated Parmesan cheese
- ⅓ cup dry roasted, salted sunflower kernels
- 6 tablespoons lemon juice
  Salt
- 5 pounds russet potatoes, peeled and cut into large pieces
- 4 cloves garlic, peeled and smashed
- 1 tablespoon kosher salt
- ¾ cup unsalted butter
- 1 cup heavy cream, half-and-half, or light cream
- 12 ounces cream cheese, softened and cut into small pieces

1. For Kale Pesto, place chopped kale leaves and stems, olive oil, garlic, Parmesan, and sunflower kernels in a food processor. Cover and process until a smooth paste forms. Blend in lemon juice and salt to taste. Thin with water, if desired. Set aside.
2. In a 6-quart pot cover potatoes and garlic with water to cover; stir in salt. Bring to boiling. Reduce heat; simmer, covered, for 20 minutes or until very tender. Drain. Return vegetables to pot.
3. While potatoes are cooking, in a small saucepan melt butter; add cream. Keep warm over low heat.
4. Mash potatoes in the cooking pot with a potato masher. Stir in the cream cheese. Slowly add the butter mixture, stirring and melting cream cheese. Potatoes may look soupy at first but will quickly absorb liquid. Season to taste with salt and pepper. Top with Kale Pesto.
PER SERVING 306 cal., 25 g fat (11 g sat. fat), 51 mg chol., 216 mg sodium, 18 g carb., 2 g fiber, 5 g pro.
Make Ahead Mashed potatoes can be made 4 hours before dinner and kept warm in a 6-quart slow cooker on low-heat setting. Stir before serving. Kale Pesto can be made up to 1 month ahead and frozen in a resealable plastic freezer bag. Thaw overnight and serve at room temperature.

Braised Cabbage with Spicy Croutons

PREP 10 minutes COOK 18 minutes
MAKES 6 servings

- 2 tablespoons olive oil
- 1 tablespoon butter
- ⅓ of a 12-ounce baguette, torn into coarse crumbs (2 cups)
- ¼ teaspoon garlic powder
- ¼ teaspoon crushed red pepper
- 1 small head green cabbage, cut into 6 wedges
  Salt and black pepper
- ½ cup water
  Snipped fresh Italian parsley
  Lemon wedges

1. For Spicy Croutons, in a very large skillet heat 1 tablespoon of the olive oil and the butter over medium-high heat. Add bread, garlic powder, and crushed red pepper. Cook and stir for 3 to 5 minutes or until golden brown. Remove croutons from skillet with slotted spoon; cool in a single layer on paper towels.
2. Add cabbage to the skillet, overlapping wedges if necessary. Sprinkle with salt and black pepper. Add the water; bring to boiling. Reduce heat; simmer, covered, about 15 minutes or until tender.
3. Place cabbage on a platter; drizzle the remaining 1 tablespoon olive oil. Sprinkle with croutons and parsley; serve with lemon wedges.
PER SERVING 141 cal., 7 g fat (2 g sat. fat), 5 mg chol., 254 mg sodium, 19 g carb., 4 g fiber, 4 g pro.

Arugula-Fennel Salad

START TO FINISH 25 minutes
MAKES 8 servings

- ¼ cup white balsamic vinegar
- ¼ cup olive oil
- 1 clove garlic, minced
- ¼ teaspoon salt
- ¼ teaspoon freshly ground black pepper
- 1 bulb fennel, trimmed, halved, and cored
- 3 cups arugula
- 1 cup cubed fresh pineapple and/or peeled orange slices
- ½ cup golden raisins

1. In a large bowl whisk together the vinegar, oil, garlic, salt, and pepper. Using a mandoline, slice fennel into bowl. Add arugula, pineapple, and raisins. Toss gently to combine.
PER SERVING 127 cal., 7 g fat (1 g sat. fat), 0 mg chol., 92 mg sodium, 17 g carb., 2 g fiber, 1 g pro.

ARUGULA-FENNEL
SALAD

GARLIC
ROSEMARY
DRESSING

Garlic Rosemary Dressing

PREP **30 minutes** CHILL **Overnight**
BAKE **25 minutes at 350°F/20 minutes
at 375°F** STAND **10 minutes**
MAKES **12 servings**

- 1 18-ounce loaf rustic white bread, cut into 1-inch cubes, about 10 cups
- 1 18-ounce loaf rustic whole wheat bread, cut into 1-inch cubes, about 10 cups
- ½ cup unsalted butter
- 2 pounds yellow onions, chopped (6½ cups)
- 6 stalks celery, chopped (3 cups)
- 2 teaspoons celery seeds
- 10 cloves garlic, minced
- 4 large eggs, beaten
- 3 tablespoons finely chopped rosemary leaves
- 2 tablespoons finely chopped sage leaves
- 3 to 4 cups turkey or chicken stock
- 2½ teaspoons salt
- 1 teaspoon freshly ground black pepper
- ¼ cup olive oil
- 2 cups fresh or frozen cranberries

1. Preheat oven to 350°F. Spread bread cubes in two shallow baking pans and toast for 15 minutes, or until lightly golden, stirring frequently. Cool.
2. In a large skillet heat butter over medium-high heat. Add onions, celery, and celery seeds. Cook and stir until soft, about 10 minutes.
3. In a very large bowl combine garlic, eggs, rosemary, and sage. Add 3 cups of the stock, salt, and pepper. Working in batches, add toasted bread cubes and cooked onion mixture; gently toss.
4. Divide dressing between two lightly greased 3-quart baking dishes. Drizzle each dish with 2 tablespoons olive oil. Cover dishes with foil; refrigerate overnight.
5. Preheat oven to 350°F. Bake dressing, covered, for 25 minutes. Remove foil and increase oven temperature to 375°F. Bake for 20 minutes or until tops are lightly browned and dressing is heated through. Sprinkle 1 cup cranberries onto dressing in each dish. Let stand 10 minutes before serving.

PER SERVING *122 cal., 5 g fat (2 g sat. fat), 25 mg chol., 306 mg sodium, 15 g carb., 2 g fiber, 4 g pro.*

Make Ahead Bread can be toasted up to 1 week ahead, cooled then stored in an airtight container. Dressing can be assembled up to 1 day ahead and refrigerated.

Blistered Green Beans

PREP **15 minutes**
ROAST **15 minutes at 450°F**
MAKES **4 servings**

- 1 pound whole slender green beans, trimmed
- 2 tablespoons olive oil
  Salt and freshly ground black pepper
- ½ cup fresh Italian parsley, coarsely chopped
- 1 large clove garlic, minced
- ½ cup roasted and salted pistachios, coarsely chopped
- 2 tablespoons thin shreds orange zest

1. Preheat oven to 450°F. Toss beans with olive oil in a 15×10×1-inch baking pan. Sprinkle with salt and pepper. Spread beans in a single layer. Roast for 15 to 20 minutes or until beans are blistered and caramelized in spots and almost tender.
2. Sprinkle beans with parsley and garlic. Top with pistachios and orange zest. Let stand at least 5 minutes before serving warm or at room temperature.

PER SERVING *193 cal., 14 g fat (2 g sat. fat), 0 mg chol., 225 mg sodium, 14 g carb., 5 g fiber, 6 g pro.*

BLISTERED GREEN BEANS

Macadamia Nut Cranberry Shortbread

PREP 1½ hours BAKE 1 hour
at 325°F COOL 2 hours
CHILL 45 minutes STAND 1 hour
MAKES 32 servings

- 1 recipe Candied Cranberries
- 4 cups all-purpose flour
- 1 cup granulated sugar
- 1 teaspoon salt
- 2 cups chilled unsalted butter
  (1 pound)
- 1 cup chopped macadamia nuts
- 1 cup white baking pieces
- ½ cup coarse white decorating
  sugar

1. Prepare Candied Cranberries. Preheat oven to 325°F. Line a 13×9×2-inch baking pan with parchment paper.
2. In a bowl stir together the flour, granulated sugar, and salt. Coarsely shred the butter over the flour mixture. Toss in with a fork. Use your fingers to gently massage the butter into the flour until the mixture resembles coarse cornmeal and sticks together when squeezed between your fingers.

MACADAMIA NUT
CRANBERRY
SHORTBREAD

3. Add the nuts, baking pieces, and Candied Cranberries; stir lightly to mix. Transfer to the prepared baking pan and press evenly. Sprinkle the top with coarse sugar. Bake for 60 to 70 minutes or until top is golden brown. Remove and cool in pan on a wire rack for at least 2 hours.
4. Remove from pan and cut into bars. Cover and store shortbread in the refrigerator up to 3 days (or in the freezer for 3 months).
Candied Cranberries In a medium saucepan combine ½ cup grapefruit juice; ½ cup cranberry juice; 1½ cups granulated sugar; half of a vanilla bean, halved lengthwise; ½ teaspoon ground cinnamon; zest of half an orange and lemon; and a pinch of salt. Cook and stir over medium heat until sugar is dissolved. Remove and cool until warm but not hot. Stir half of one 12-ounce package thawed frozen cranberries. Let stand until room temperature. Transfer to a bowl; cover and chill overnight. Drain cranberries well, reserving syrup and vanilla bean. Cover and chill the syrup with the vanilla bean up to 3 weeks. Toss cranberries with ¼ cup white granulated sugar. Spread cranberries in a single-player on a shallow parchment paper-lined baking pan. Let stand for 1 hour to dry. Store loosely covered at room temperature up to 1 week.

PER SERVING 275 cal., 17 g fat
(10 g sat. fat), 31 mg chol., 85 mg sodium,
29 g carb., 1 g fiber, 2 g pro.

Hazelnut Truffle Cake

PREP 30 minutes
BAKE 1¼ hours at 350°F
COOL 1 hour CHILL 3 hours
MAKES 12 servings

- 6 eggs
- ¼ cup packed brown sugar
- 2 tablespoons Frangelico or other hazelnut liqueur
- 1 13-ounce jar chocolate-hazelnut spread
- ½ cup butter, melted and cooled
- ½ cup finely ground hazelnuts (filberts)
- 2 ounces unsweetened chocolate, melted
- 2 tablespoons unsweetened cocoa powder
- ½ teaspoon salt
- ½ cup heavy cream
- 1 tablespoon granulated sugar
- 2 teaspoons heavy cream
  Toasted chopped hazelnuts (filberts) (tip, page 64) (optional)

1. Preheat oven to 350°F. Butter a 9-inch springform pan. Line bottom of pan with parchment paper. Tightly wrap outside of pan with heavy foil.
2. In a large mixing bowl beat eggs, brown sugar, and 1 tablespoon of the Frangelico with a mixer on medium to high for 4 to 6 minutes or until pale and thickened. Reserve 1 tablespoon of the chocolate-hazelnut spread. In a medium bowl combine the remaining chocolate-hazelnut spread and melted butter. Stir butter mixture into egg mixture. Stir in ground hazelnuts, melted chocolate, cocoa powder, and salt. Spread batter in the springform pan.
3. Place springform pan in a shallow roasting pan. Place roasting pan on oven rack. Pour enough hot water into the roasting pan to reach halfway up sides of springform pan. Bake for 1¼ hours (center should be set and top dry to the touch).
4. Carefully remove springform pan from water; remove foil from pan. Cool cake in pan on a wire rack for 15 minutes. Loosen cake from sides of pan; cool for 45 minutes more. Remove sides of pan. Cover and chill at least 3 hours before serving.
5. In a medium mixing bowl beat ½ cup cream, granulated sugar, and the remaining Frangelico on medium until soft peaks form (tips curl). In a small bowl whisk together the reserved chocolate-hazelnut spread and 2 teaspoons cream.
6. Serve cake slices with whipped cream. If desired, sprinkle with chopped hazelnuts and drizzle with chocolate-hazelnut cream.

PER SERVING 383 cal., 28 g fat
(13 g sat. fat), 128 mg chol., 219 mg sodium,
28 g carb., 2 g fiber, 7 g pro.

HAZELNUT TRUFFLE
CAKE

KALE AND WHITE BEAN
SOUP, PAGE 152

Casual Noshing

HOLIDAY HOUSEGUESTS add to the fun of the season. When they arrive at your doorstep, be prepared with quick-to-fix foods that fit into your busy schedule. These easy-on-the-cook soups, sandwiches, salads, casseroles, and sweets are simple and delicious.

Ultimate Grilled Cheese and Ham Panini with Parsnip Fries

PREP 25 minutes COOK 6 minutes
MAKES 4 servings

- 1 16-ounce loaf unsliced ciabatta or Italian bread or 8 slices French, sourdough, multigrain, or oatmeal bread, sliced ½ to ¾ inch thick
- ½ cup chutney, any flavor
- 3 ounces thinly sliced Fontina, Jarlsberg, Gruyére, or Swiss cheese
- 8 ounces thinly sliced cooked ham
- 1 small Bosc or Anjou pear or 1 small apple, cored and thinly sliced
- 1 cup fresh baby arugula or spinach
- 3 ounces thinly sliced Gouda, Edam, Muenster, or provolone cheese
- 2 to 3 tablespoons butter, softened, or olive oil
- 1 recipe Parsnip Fries or potato chips (optional)

1. If using bread loaf, carefully trim off the top crust of bread to make a flat surface, if necessary. Turn bread over; trim off bottom crust, if necessary. Cut remaining bread loaf in half horizontally for two ½-inch-thick slices.

2. Preheat an electric sandwich press, a covered indoor grill, a grill pan, or a 12-inch skillet over medium-low heat for 1 to 2 minutes.

3. If needed, snip any large pieces of chutney. Spread chutney on one side of each slice of bread. Place the Fontina cheese on half the loaf or on four of the bread slices. Top with ham, pear, arugula, the Gouda cheese, and the other half of bread loaf or remaining slices. Spread both sides of loaf or sandwiches with butter or brush with oil. Cut loaf crosswise into four sandwiches.

4. Place sandwiches (two at a time, if necessary) in the sandwich press or indoor grill. Cover and cook for 6 to 8 minutes or until bread is toasted and cheese is melted. (If using a grill pan or skillet, place sandwiches in pan. Weight sandwiches down with a heavy skillet. Cook until bread is lightly toasted. Using hot pads, carefully remove top skillet. Turn sandwiches, weight down, and cook until bread is toasted and cheese is melted. If desired, serve with Parsnip Fries or potato chips.

PER SERVING *659 cal., 25 g fat (14 g sat. fat), 101 mg chol., 1,867 mg sodium, 78 g carb., 4 g fiber, 30 g pro.*

Parsnip Fries Peel 4 medium parsnips; cut into ⅛-inch lengthwise slices using a mandolin or cut by hand. Place parsnip slices in a large bowl of ice water; soak for 10 minutes. Thoroughly drain parsnips; pat dry with paper towels. In a 3-quart saucepan or an electric deep-fat fryer, heat 2 inches of vegetable or peanut oil to 375°F. Fry parsnips, one-fourth at a time, about 1 to 2 minutes or until golden brown and crisp. Remove parsnips from hot oil using a slotted spoon; drain on paper towels. Sprinkle with kosher salt. Transfer parsnips to a wire rack set on a baking sheet, arranging them in a single layer. Keep warm in a 300°F oven.

Apple Pork Ragu

START TO FINISH 45 minutes
MAKES 6 servings

- 12 ounces lean boneless pork, cut in 1-inch pieces
- 1 medium onion, halved and thinly sliced
- 2 cloves garlic, minced
- 1 tablespoon olive oil
- ¼ cup apple cider
- 2 tablespoons tomato paste
- 2 apples, such as Honey Crisp, cored and chopped
- 1 14.5-ounce can diced tomatoes
- 1 cup chicken broth
- ¼ cup pimiento-stuffed green olives, coarsely chopped
- ¼ cup chopped fresh Italian parsley
  Cooked polenta
  Finely shredded Parmesan cheese

1. In a 4-quart Dutch oven cook pork, onion, and garlic in hot oil over medium-high heat about 5 minutes or until browned. Add apple cider. Cook and stir, scraping up any browned bits from the Dutch oven, until the cider is nearly evaporated. Stir in tomato paste. Cook and stir 1 minute more.

2. Stir in apples, undrained tomatoes, and broth; bring to boiling. Reduce heat; simmer, uncovered, for 15 minutes. Remove from heat. Stir in olives and parsley. Serve warm over cooked polenta. Sprinkle with Parmesan.

PER SERVING *161 cal., 5 g fat (1 g sat. fat), 38 mg chol., 434 mg sodium, 16 g carb., 3 g fiber, 13 g pro.*

ULTIMATE GRILLED CHEESE AND HAM PANINI WITH PARSNIP FRIES

APPLE PORK
RAGU

TUSCAN TUNA MAC
CASEROLE

3. Remove from heat and stir in cheese and 1½ tablespoons of the Tuscan Garlic Herb Blend, and ¼ teaspoon each salt and pepper. Fold in the noodles, tuna, and 3 tablespoons of the basil. Spread in prepared dish and arrange tomato slices in a single layer.

4. In a small bowl combine bread crumbs; remaining 2 tablespoons butter, melted; remaining ½ tablespoon herb mix, and remaining salt and pepper. Sprinkle over tomatoes. Bake for 30 minutes or until bubbly and crumbs are golden brown. Sprinkle with remaining basil.

Tuscan Garlic Herb Blend In a small bowl combine 2 tablespoons dried rosemary, crushed; 2 tablespoons dried thyme, crushed; 4 teaspoons fennel seeds; 4 teaspoons garlic powder; 2 teaspoons dried marjoram, crushed; and 1 teaspoon dried sage, crushed.

PER SERVING *485 cal., 26 g fat (13 g sat. fat), 109 mg chol., 700 mg sodium, 36 g carb., 3 g fiber, 27 g pro.*

Kale and White Bean Soup

(photo page 149)

START TO FINISH **25 minutes**
MAKES **4 servings**

- ½ cup chopped carrot
- ½ cup sliced celery
- ½ cup chopped onion
- 1 tablespoon olive oil
- 4 cups reduced-sodium chicken broth
- 4 cups chopped kale
- 1 15- to 19-ounce can cannellini beans, rinsed and drained
- 1 14.5-ounce can stewed or diced tomatoes with basil, garlic, and oregano, undrained
  Salt and black pepper
- 1 cup croutons
  Grated Parmesan cheese (optional)

1. In a large saucepan cook carrot, celery, and onion in hot oil over medium-high heat for 3 minutes, stirring occasionally. Add broth, kale, beans, and tomatoes. Bring to boiling; reduce heat. Cover and simmer for 10 minutes, stirring once. Season to taste with salt and pepper.

Tuscan Tuna Mac Casserole

PREP **40 minutes**
BAKE **30 minutes at 375°F**
MAKES **6 servings**

  Nonstick cooking spray
- 6 tablespoons butter
- 1 cup sliced cremini mushrooms
- ½ cup finely chopped red and/or green sweet peppers
- ¼ cup finely chopped onion
- ¼ cup all-purpose flour
- 2½ cups milk
- 4 ounces fontina cheese, shredded (1 cup)
- 2 tablespoons Tuscan Garlic Herb Blend

- ½ teaspoon salt
- ½ teaspoon ground black pepper
- 3 cups cooked egg noodles
- 2 5- to 6-ounce cans oil-packed tuna, drained
- ¼ cup chopped fresh basil
- 1 tomato, sliced
- ½ cup panko bread crumbs

1. Preheat oven to 375°F. Coat a 2-quart gratin or baking dish with cooking spray.

2. Melt 4 tablespoons of the butter in a 3-quart saucepan over medium heat. Add mushrooms, peppers, and onion. Cook and stir for 5 minutes or until softened. Stir in flour and cook for 1 minute. Stir in milk until smooth. Cook until thickened and bubbly.

2. Divide croutons among four shallow bowls. Ladle soup into bowls and, if desired, sprinkle with cheese.

PER SERVING *245 cal., 4 g fat (1 g sat. fat), 0 mg chol., 1,155 mg sodium, 41 g carb., 8 g fiber, 15 g pro.*

Date- and Balsamic- Glazed Brussels Sprouts

PREP **25 minutes**
ROAST **20 minutes at 425°F**
MAKES **8 servings**

2 pounds Brussels sprouts
1 tablespoon olive oil
2 teaspoons butter
3 cloves garlic, minced
⅓ cup balsamic vinegar
¼ cup whole pitted dates, chopped
¼ teaspoon salt
⅛ teaspoon black pepper

1. Preheat oven to 425°F. Trim stems and remove any wilted outer leaves from Brussels sprouts; wash. Halve Brussels sprouts; spread in a single layer in a 15×10×1-inch baking pan. Drizzle oil over Brussels sprouts. Roast 20 to 25 minutes or until crisp-tender, stirring once or twice.
2. Meanwhile, for sauce, in a large nonstick skillet melt butter over medium heat. Add garlic; cook 30 seconds. Add balsamic vinegar, dates, salt, and pepper. Cook 5 to 7 minutes or until sauce is thickened and reduced to about ¼ cup. Add roasted sprouts to the sauce in skillet.

PER SERVING *99 cal., 3 g fat (1 g sat. fat), 3 mg chol., 112 mg sodium, 17 g carb., 5 g fiber, 4 g pro.*

Avocado and Roasted Carrot Salad

PREP **20 minutes**
ROAST **20 minutes at 425°F**
MAKES **16 servings**

1 pound carrots, cut into bite-size strips
1 tablespoon olive oil
 Salt and black pepper
3 avocados, halved, seeded, peeled, and sliced
⅓ cup red wine vinegar
¼ cup extra virgin olive oil

½ teaspoon kosher salt
½ teaspoon dried oregano, crushed
¼ teaspoon cracked black pepper
2 5-ounce packages torn mixed greens
¾ cup green onions, thinly sliced
6 ounces, queso fresco, crumbled (1½ cups)

1. Preheat oven to 425°F. Place carrots in a shallow roasting pan; toss with the 1 tablespoon oil. Sprinkle lightly with salt and pepper. Roast, uncovered, for 15 to 20 minutes or just until tender, stirring once. Cool in pan on wire rack.

2. For dressing, place half of one avocado in a medium bowl and mash with a fork until smooth. Whisk vinegar, oil, salt, oregano, and pepper into mashed avocado.
3. In a very large bowl combine greens, remaining avocados, roasted carrots, green onions, and queso fresco. Add dressing and toss to combine.

PER SERVING *129 cal., 11 g fat (3 g sat. fat), 7 mg chol., 167 mg sodium, 6 g carb., 3 g fiber, 3 g pro.*

AVOCADO AND ROASTED CARROT SALAD

Pumpkin Bars with Marcona Almonds

PREP 25 minutes
BAKE 40 minutes at 350°F
MAKES 16 servings

- ½ cup unsalted butter, melted and cooled
- 1 cup packed dark brown sugar
- 1 egg
- 2 teaspoons vanilla
- 1 cup canned pumpkin
- 1½ cups all-purpose flour
- 1½ teaspoons ground cinnamon
- ½ teaspoon baking powder
- ½ teaspoon ground ginger
- ¼ teaspoon salt
- ¼ teaspoon ground allspice
- ¼ teaspoon ground nutmeg
- 1½ cups roasted and salted marcona almonds, coarsely chopped
  Sweetened whipped cream (optional)
  Maple syrup (optional)
  Mint leaves (optional)

1. Preheat oven to 350°F. Grease a 9-inch square baking pan, line with parchment paper, and grease the paper; set pan aside.
2. In a medium bowl stir together butter and sugar until no lumps remain. Stir in egg and vanilla. Stir in pumpkin. Add flour, cinnamon, baking powder, ginger, salt, allspice, and nutmeg; stir until combined and no pockets of flour remain. Fold in half the almonds. Spoon into pan, spreading to edges. Top with remaining almonds.
3. Bake for 40 minutes or until a wooden toothpick inserted near center comes out clean. Cool in pan on a wire rack. Use parchment paper to lift uncut bars from pan. Remove from paper and cut into bars. Top with sweetened whipped cream. If desired, drizzle with maple syrup and sprinkle with mint leaves.

PER SERVING 233 cal., 13 g fat (4 g sat. fat), 27 mg chol., 63 mg sodium, 26 g carb., 3 g fiber, 5 g pro.

Christmas Pudding Mug Cake

START TO FINISH 15 minutes
MAKES 3 servings

  Nonstick cooking spray
- ½ cup dried cranberries
- 1 tablespoon orange juice
- ½ of a 10.3-ounce loaf frozen gingerbread-flavor pound cake*
- 3 tablespoons butter, melted
- 1 egg
- 1 teaspoon vanilla
- ½ teaspoon baking powder
- ¼ teaspoon kosher salt
- ¼ cup butter, softened
- ¼ cup powdered sugar
- 1 teaspoon bourbon or vanilla
- 3 dark sweet cherries with stems (optional)

1. Coat the inside of three 6-ounce microwave-safe mugs with nonstick cooking spray; set aside. Place cranberries and orange juice in large microwave-safe bowl and heat on high for 30 seconds. Set aside.
2. Cut cake into 2-inch pieces. Place cake in a food processor. Cover and process until crumbs form. Add 3 tablespoons butter, egg, vanilla, baking powder, and salt. Cover and process until a batter forms. Stir batter into cranberry mixture.
3. Spoon batter into mugs. Microwave on high for 2 minutes or until a toothpick inserted near the center comes out clean.
4. Meanwhile, for the bourbon hard sauce, in a small bowl combine the ¼ cup butter, powdered sugar, and bourbon. Stir just until combined. Serve cake warm topped with bourbon hard sauce and cherries, if desired.

PER SERVING 542 cal., 34 g fat (20 g sat. fat), 160 mg chol., 707 mg sodium, 54 g carb., 2 g fiber, 4 g pro.

* If you do not find the gingerbread-flavor pound cake, substitute half of a 10.75-ounce loaf pound cake, adding ⅛ teaspoon each ground ginger and ground cinnamon.

PUMPKIN BARS
WITH MARCONA
ALMONDS

CHRISTMAS
PUDDING
MUG CAKE

INDEX